First published in 1963 by Chatto & Windus Limited
Published in 2003, in this format, by
PEN & SWORD MILITARY CLASSICS
*an imprint of*
Pen & Sword Books Limited
47, Church Street
Barnsley
S. Yorkshire
S70 2AS

ISBN 0 85052 963 8

A CIP record for this book is
available from the British Library

Printed in England by
CPI UK

# STRIKE HARD, STRIKE SURE

*Epics of the Bombers*

RALPH BARKER

PEN & SWORD MILITARY CLASSICS

# STRIKE HARD, STRIKE SURE

Many thousands of words have been written, and many more uttered, about the conception of the bomber offensive in World War II, the strategy and tactics of Bomber Command, the choice of target systems, the methods of attack, the evaluation of bombing results and the implications for the national war effort, both Allied and enemy. Surprisingly little has been told of the men who flew these bombers, who faced and sustained a loss rate never before borne by a military force of comparable size in history. Here at last is the story of some of those men, and of the stirring actions in which they took part. What is known about the daylight Lancaster raid which penetrated at roof-top level to the submarine-engine factory at Augsburg on 17 April 1942? Who today remembers Nettleton? What was achieved by the sacrifice of the Battles of 12 Squadron against the Maastricht Bridges during the blitzkreig, for which two young regular airmen named Garland and Gray were posthumously awarded the VC? What happened on Guy Gibson's last flight? What was the ordeal of the young Highlander who fought the flames in a blazing bomber to rescue his comrades and who was so badly burned that his own skipper failed to recognize him? Who was the introspective young outback Australian whose devotion to duty in the face of overwhelming odds is said to be unsurpassed in the annals of the Royal Air Force? Who conceived the fantastic idea of climbing out on to the wing of a Lancaster at 20,000 feet over Germany to extinguish a fire?

These are only a few of the incredible stories of heroism and sacrifice which make this book a worthy tribute to the men of the bombers, and to the contribution that they made to the fall of Nazi Germany.

# PEN & SWORD MILITARY CLASSICS

We hope you enjoy your Pen and Sword Military Classic. The series is designed to give readers quality military history at affordable prices. Below is a list of the titles that are planned for 2003. Pen and Sword Classics are available from all good bookshops. If you would like to keep in touch with further developments in the series, including information on the Classics Club, then please contact Pen and Sword at the address below.

## 2003 List

**Series No.**

| | | |
|---|---|---|
| | **JANUARY** | |
| 1 | The Bowmen of England | Donald Featherstone |
| 2 | The Life & Death of the Afrika Korps | Ronald Lewin |
| 3 | The Old Front Line | John Masefield |
| 4 | Wellington & Napoleon | Robin Neillands |
| | **FEBRUARY** | |
| 5 | Beggars in Red | John Strawson |
| 6 | The Luftwaffe: A History | John Killen |
| 7 | Siege: Malta 1940–1943 | Ernle Bradford |
| | **MARCH** | |
| 8 | Hitler as Military Commander | John Strawson |
| 9 | Nelson's Battles | Oliver Warner |
| 10 | The Western Front 1914–1918 | John Terraine |
| | **APRIL** | |
| 11 | The Killing Ground | Tim Travers |
| 12 | Vimy | Pierre Berton |
| | **MAY** | |
| 13 | Dictionary of the First World War | Pope & Wheal |
| 14 | 1918: The Last Act | Barrie Pitt |
| | **JUNE** | |
| 15 | Hitler's Last Offensive | Peter Elstob |
| 16 | Naval Battles of World War Two | Geoffrey Bennett |
| | **JULY** | |
| 17 | Omdurman | Philip Ziegler |
| 18 | Strike Hard, Strike Sure | Ralph Barker |
| | **AUGUST** | |
| 19 | The Black Angels | Rupert Butler |
| 20 | The Black Ship | Dudley Pope |
| | **SEPTEMBER** | |
| 21 | The Argentine Fight for the Falklands | Martin Middlebrook |
| 22 | The Narrow Margin | Wood & Dempster |
| | **OCTOBER** | |
| 23 | Warfare in the Age of Bonaparte | Michael Glover |
| 24 | With the German Guns | Herbert Sulzbach |
| | **NOVEMBER** | |
| 25 | Dictionary of the Second World War | Pope & Wheal |
| 26 | Not Ordinary Men | John Colvin |

## PEN AND SWORD BOOKS LTD

47 Church Street • Barnsley • South Yorkshire • S70 2AS

### Tel: 01226 734555 • 734222

**E-mail:** enquiries@pen-and-sword.co.uk • **Website:** www.pen-and-sword.co.uk

# Contents

# LIST OF PLATES

# ACKNOWLEDGEMENTS

I SHOULD like to acknowledge, first and foremost, my very great indebtedness to the survivors of the various actions described in this collection of stories. Without their generous help I should have been able to add little to official accounts.

I am also indebted to various departments of the Air Ministry, and especially to the Air Historical Branch, the Information Division, and the Air Ministry Library, whose staffs have greatly assisted in finding records which have enabled me to get the authentic background to the stories.

For other factual background I have drawn on Guy Gibson's account of the dam-busting raid in *Enemy Coast Ahead* (Michael Joseph) and on Paul Brickhill's *The Dam Busters* (Evans), while for most of the material on Gibson's last flight I am indebted to Mr G. J. Zwanenburg, of Amsterdam, and to the Burgomaster of Steenbergen. I have drawn on Colonel Livry Level's and Remy's *The Gates Burst Open* (Arco) and Sir Basil Embry's *Mission Completed* (Methuen) for background detail to the attack on Amiens prison, and I am greatly indebted to M. Henri Moisan, of Amiens, for his account of the attack itself.

A source of background information on many of the stories has been *Royal Air Force 1939–1945*, by Denis Richards and Hilary St G. Saunders (HMSO), and I have also consulted *No. 5 Group*, by W. J. Lawrence (Faber).

I must record my gratitude to the Commander-in-Chief and Officers of Bomber Command for enabling me to see at first hand a part of the work of the V-Force, described in the Epilogue.

Grateful acknowledgement is also made to *Planet News, Illustrated,* and The Imperial War Museum for permission to reproduce the following photographs :

Page 1    John Garwell – Private source
             'Flap' Sherwood – Imperial War Museum

Page 2    Imperial War Museum

Page 3    Private sources

Page 4    Donald Garland – Imperial War Museum
             Remainder from private sources

Page 5    Hughie Edwards – *Illustrated*
             Remainder from Imperial War Museum

Page 6    Norman Jackson – *Planet News*
             Remainder from Imperial War Museum

Page 7    Bill Reid and Les Rolton – Private sources
             Remainder from Imperial War Museum

Page 8    Imperial War Museum

R. B.

# 1

## *Daylight over Augsburg*

ON 22 February 1942, Air Marshal Arthur T. Harris took over as Commander-in-Chief, Bomber Command. Ten days later, on 2 March, the first two Lancaster squadrons, Nos. 44 and 97, became operational. The arrival of the new Commander, who was to retain his appointment until the end of the war and to become one of the war's most controversial figures, thus coincided with the introduction of a new offensive weapon, the four-engined Avro Lancaster, destined to prove the greatest of all the bombers of the Second World War.

The new Commander-in-Chief was given a clear directive by the Air Ministry on the employment of his force. This directive called in effect for the area bombing of industrial towns, the chief object being to destroy Germany's capacity and will to wage war. But it did not altogether rule out the occasional pinpoint attack against a specially selected target, and Harris was naturally keen to test the new Lancaster in this role.

In March 1942 there came a significant exchange of telegrams between Churchill and Roosevelt. The situation on all fronts was bleak. In Russia, in North Africa, in Asia, and in the Pacific, the Allies were defending desperately or in full retreat. Yet to the British – and, in the long run, to the whole Allied cause – none of these fronts presented a more mortal threat than that contained in the U-Boat offensive in the Atlantic. This was the one weapon with which Germany could still knock Britain out of the war. And without the existence of Britain as a base, there could be no round-the-clock Anglo-American bomber offensive and no effective second front.

The entry of the United States into the war in December 1941 had only served to spread the U-Boat menace. With the Americans preoccupied in the Pacific, terrible havoc was wrought by the U-Boats along the Atlantic Coast. One hundred and seventeen ships totalling over three-quarters of a million tons were sunk in the Atlantic in the first two months of 1942, the worst losses of the war so far. And in the months that followed, the ravages of the U-boats, particularly in American waters, brought us to the brink of disaster.

Churchill suggested a number of drastic naval measures to Roosevelt and the President agreed. But a few days later Roosevelt, alarmed by further catastrophic losses and exasperated, perhaps, by gratuitous British advice, called on Churchill for decisive British action against the sources of U-Boat strength.

Air Marshal Harris, although not responsible for the area bombing directive, had quickly become the fiercest advocate of it. But he could not ignore the clamour that demanded immediate action to alleviate the terrible massacres of shipping in the Atlantic.

Pinpoint targets such as factories, submarine yards and pens could not be located at night with any certainty, and even if they could be found there was little confidence in our ability to hit them with the help of the bombing aids then available. Certainly none of the bombers in service up to that time could hope to survive over Germany by day. But what about the Lancaster? Might it not be possible that the speed, range and armament of the new Lancaster would enable it to thrust deep into enemy territory by day, delivering pinpoint attacks from low level against specially selected targets?

Harris instructed his planning staffs to select a target whose destruction might put a severe brake on the production and refitting of U-Boats, and to report on the feasibility of attacking such a target from low level in daylight with the new Lancaster. The target they selected was the MAN

Diesel-Engine Works at Augsburg, Bavaria. This was the largest diesel-engine factory in Germany, believed to be producing half the total requirement for large submarines as well as various engines for warships, tanks and lorries. Its destruction, or partial destruction, followed by similar blows against other vital targets, might help to reduce the mounting numbers of U-Boats putting to sea and restrict German submarine warfare for a long time to come.

The attacking of what became known as 'panacea' targets – targets whose destruction could be reckoned to have an immediate effect on some aspect of Germany's ability to make war – was a policy to which Harris himself was bitterly opposed. But the disastrous losses in the Atlantic demanded flexibility. And it was possible that in the Lancaster Britain had produced a weapon which called for some adjustment to the area bombing policy. It must be put to the test.

The appreciation by the planning staffs at Bomber Command dealt first with the fighter opposition that might be encountered. It was known that about half the fighter strength of the *Luftwaffe* was operating on the Russian front. A further quarter was pinned down in the Middle East and the Balkans. Thus, in spite of feverish efforts to recuperate, German fighter strength in the West was running at a much lower figure than a year earlier. It remained a formidable force, but in the opinion of the planners it was inadequate to cover a length of coastline that exceeded 2000 miles.

The bulk of this force was disposed in the Pas de Calais area and in Norway. Other coastal areas were covered by meagre fighter forces and inland areas were protected still less. Even such fighter forces as existed in these areas were inferior in ability and determination to the units in the Pas de Calais. And the night fighter force was disposed almost exclusively in North-West Germany and Holland.

As yet there was no British or Allied fighter capable of escorting bombers for a fraction of the distance involved. But against this the new Lancaster carried a powerful defensive armament and was capable of comparatively high speeds.

Operating in formation, as they could in daylight, the combined fire-power of a section of three Lancasters was thought to be sufficient to deter all but the most aggressive enemy fighter pilots, while their speed would present a difficult interception problem.

The most serious danger obviously came from the fighters in the Pas de Calais. But if this threat could be accounted for in a well co-ordinated diversionary operation, the planners concluded that the qualities of the Lancaster would enable a formation to cross the coast of France in daylight at a weak point and strike deep into the southern interior of Germany without meeting serious opposition. Vital targets such as the diesel-engine works at Augsburg, hitherto immune from attack owing to distance and to difficulties of recognition at night, could thus be bombed with precision.

There were two further recommendations. The enemy coast should be crossed at low level to avoid radar detection, and the attack should be made at dusk so that the return journey, with enemy defences alerted, could be made under cover of darkness.

This was how the operation looked to the planners. To the crews of the squadrons concerned it looked rather different.

Seven crews from No. 44 (Rhodesia) Squadron at Waddington, and seven from No. 97 Squadron at Woodhall, were singled out for special training. The seventh aircraft in each squadron was a reserve in case someone fell out. Nearly all the crews were experienced men at the start of their second operational tour.

On 14 April each squadron started practising formation flying, independently as yet, but giving rise to insistent rumours that some big daylight raid was in the offing. Next day the crews were briefed for a long low-level cross-country flight over England and Scotland of five to six hours' duration, and for the first time the members of each squadron learnt that they were to operate with another squadron. A combined attack on a heavily defended target now looked a certainty.

They flew south to Selsey Bill independently, then joined forces and turned north for Lincoln and Falkirk before simulating a low-level attack on the town of Inverness. Then back to their bases after a round trip of over a thousand miles. Low-level formation flying was not without its dangers – or its exhilaration. Mostly the crews enjoyed themselves. But speculation was rife as to what the target might be. Most men thought it must be one of the big German ships – *Scharnhorst, Gneisenau,* or *Tirpitz* – or perhaps some inland target in Scandinavia. Fortunately for their peace of mind, no one got anywhere near the truth.

On 16 April the crews were told that the raid would probably take place next day. They were still in complete ignorance of the target. They were confined to camp, forbidden to phone their wives, forbidden even to have a drink. Someone, it seemed, was deadly seriously about this raid.

Next morning they air-tested their aircraft. All went well except for a number of stoppages in the guns. Some of these were cleared in the air, others by the ground armourers. At length all seven aircraft in each squadron were pronounced serviceable.

Briefing was at eleven o'clock. At Woodhall, the 97 Squadron base, the crews sat down in the briefing room in an atmosphere of eager but fearful expectancy. Much the same thing was happening simultaneously at Waddington. Being kept in ignorance of the target for the past few days had been a severe nervous strain. Now at least they would know the worst.

On the wall at the far end of the briefing room at Woodhall was a single map of Western Europe, and on this map some wag had stretched a length of tape right across Northern France south of Paris, skirting northern Switzerland and into Bavaria, stopping some thirty miles north-west of Munich at a place called Augsburg. All the tension of the last few days was released in the roar of laughter that greeted this practical joke.

Before the laughter had died down, the squadron commander, Wing Commander Collier, entered and walked quietly forward to the front of the briefing room and mounted the dais. The crews came to order at once, listening intently.

'Well, gentlemen,' smiled the wing commander, 'now you know what the target is.'

But they didn't. Puzzled, they frowned back at the wing commander, waiting to hear some clue that would give them the answer. And when he inclined his head for a moment, as though to look back over his shoulder at the map, it was suddenly borne in upon them that the joke which had been the best laugh for days was no joke at all. The target must indeed be Augsburg.

That they might be asked to fly for 500 miles at low level in broad daylight over Occupied Europe, to a target in the heart of Southern Germany, had never occurred to them. Even their blackest nightmares had not foretold it. Such a thing was suicide in April 1942. But the studied gaiety of the wing commander helped to convince them.

He produced drawings and photographs of the target, and then filled in the background of the U-Boat war, leaving the crews in no doubt that a sacrifice was being demanded of them.

'The vital area of the target,' said Collier, 'covers some 600 by 300 yards and comprises the main diesel-engine shop, cylinder machinery plant, crankshaft turning and grinding equipment and the main testing and assembly shops.

'Aircraft from each squadron are to fly in two sections of three, keeping within supporting distance. If touch is lost between sections or squadrons they are to proceed independently. If one aircraft is forced to turn back in the early stages of the flight, the whole section of three will return to base.

'To ensure as far as possible that all four sections are within supporting distance in case of fighter interception during the flight across the Channel and to the south of Paris, a time of departure from Selsey Bill will be given for all aircraft.

'The period immediately after the crossing of the French coast presents the greatest danger from fighters, and to counteract this a massive diversionary operation is being mounted, involving thirty Boston bombers and some 800 fighters. They will attack airfields and other targets in the Pas de Calais, Rouen and Cherbourg areas ten minutes before you cross the coast. This should take care of the German fighters. And once you've penetrated a hundred miles into France you can expect a clear run to the target.

'Your route is from here to Selsey Bill, then to Dives-sur-Mer, where you cross the French coast, and on through Sens and Ludwigshafen to the north end of the Ammer See, where you will make a wide left-hand turn and head straight for the target. The latter part of the route, as far as the Ammer See, is pointed at Munich with the object of deceiving the enemy into thinking that the attack is aimed at that city.

'The route crosses some high ground between Sens and Ludwigshafen and section leaders are to use their own discretion in making short detours to avoid the highest points, following the general run of the valleys where practicable. Towns and defended areas are deliberately avoided by this route.

'Sections should be opened out to about three miles between each section before reaching the Ammer See. After the wide left-hand turn you will cross a light railway, and later a main railway line and a river will give you an easily recognisable lead in to the target.' Collier indicated all these landmarks on the map. 'Attacks are to be made by individual sections in formation, from as low a level as possible consistent with accurate navigation, each aircraft dropping four 1000-pound bombs in salvo with eleven-second delays.

'Take-off will be at 15.00 hours, and times of setting course from Selsey Bill have been calculated so that the first wave will reach the target at about 20.15, or shortly before dusk.

The return route will be direct from the target to base unless the remaining daylight necessitates a withdrawal to the south-west.

'Navigation, signals, intelligence and met. briefing follow. But first I want to repeat what I said at the beginning.' He paused, searching for the right words. 'I can't emphasise too strongly the vital importance of destroying this target. It's literally a matter of life and death in our struggle against the U-Boats. That's all.'

The remaining briefing was mostly detail, except that the intelligence officer gave them a piece of advice that they had never heard before. 'If you're shot down in France and manage to escape,' he said, 'make for the Black Cat Café in Bordeaux. If you get back all right, forget you ever heard of it.'

No one had ever felt it worth while to take the risk of giving such information before – a direct tie-up with the French underground. It looked as though they were being written off from the start.

Nobody ate much lunch, and as the truth penetrated, and the certainty grew that no one could possibly get back, the crews felt a gradual dulling of their fears, and a sense of fatalism crept over them. They hadn't expected to survive the war anyway. Surviving a second tour in any case had seemed unlikely. Yet in the back of their minds they stored the thought that somebody always got away with it. It would just have to be them.

Normally they weren't much impressed by stories that the destruction of a particular target might win or save the war. They were accustomed to doing the best they could, from a sense of duty, from comradeship, and from fear of failure; and they were suspicious of what they termed bull-sessions and pep-talk. Commanders obviously had to think up a good reason when they were sending you to certain death. And they had heard it all before. But the U-Boat threat was something different. The privations of the merchant seamen appalled them; calm routine endurance of the perils of the sea was something which they recognised as demanding a courage higher than their own.

So for once they put their protective cynicism aside and accepted the raid at its face value. Whatever happened they'd have a damn good crack at it, make themselves felt, go out in a blaze of glory. They'd smash that diesel-engine shop at Augsburg if it was the last thing they did. It probably would be.

Chosen to lead the raid was Squadron Leader John Nettleton of 44 Squadron, a twenty-five-year-old South African, dark-haired but fair-skinned, tall and reticent, grandson of an Admiral, born in Natal. On leaving school he had trained for the merchant service and subsequently spent eighteen months at sea, but in 1938, on a visit to England with his mother, he decided to join the RAF.

He was an inspired choice as leader. He had the naval background, and understood the hazards faced by merchant seamen. And, unlike all the other pilots on the raid, he was still on his first operational tour, retaining the boldness and freshness of outlook which was essential to dynamic leadership. Only a very few men retained this outlook throughout a second tour. Behind him he would have the impetus of experienced men, men who nevertheless accepted him readily as leader. In retrospect the choice of Nettleton, probably quite fortuitous, seems a stroke of psychological genius.

Leading the second flight of six Lancasters was Squadron Leader 'Flap' Sherwood, fair-haired and aesthetic-looking, only just twenty-three. In his desire to infuse his crews with his own fanatical keenness he often tried to panic them into a sense of urgency, hence the nickname 'Flap'.

If anyone had been in any doubt about the dangers of the raid, the attitude of those who were not going would have dispelled it. For a few hours the crews lived in a roseate, Utopian world. It was astonishing how nice to them everyone suddenly became.

Before take-off many of the men wrote letters to their sweethearts and mothers which they propped up prominently in their lockers. If they got back, the letters would be furtively torn up.

On the way out to dispersal in the squadron truck, Nettleton discussed with his No. 2, Flying Officer John Garwell, the tactics to be employed in the event of fighter interception. 'It would be disastrous to take evasive action,' said Nettleton. 'That would only result in collision and put one or two or all of us into the ground.' Garwell agreed. 'The only thing to do is to press straight on and keep flat on the ground. If anyone gets really crippled I suggest he throttles back and belly-lands straight ahead.' The word was passed round to the other crews – Warrant Officer Rhodes, Nettleton's No. 3, and the second section consisting of Flight Lieutenant Sandford, Warrant Officer Crum and Warrant Officer Beckett.

The six Lancasters all got away safely from Waddington, formed up over the airfield, and set course for Selsey Bill. The whole station came out on to the tarmac to see them off. 'Come on,' said someone, when the last Lancaster had disappeared to the south, 'let's go and have a drink. We shan't see *them* again.'

At Woodhall there was a snag. Rodley, the reserve pilot, had tagged along behind the other six throughout training. At briefing he had been appalled when the target was named, but he and his crew had clung to the hope that they were only the reserve. Then, as they watched the other six aircraft starting up, some of them began to have mixed feelings.

They had collected their parachutes, their bars of chocolate, their oranges, their thermos of coffee, and gone out to the aircraft with the rest. There they had watered the tail-wheel just in case, kicked the tyres, had a good look round for leaks, checked everything they could, and strapped themselves in. When the coloured cartridge signal was fired (R/T and W/T silence were ordered), Rodley had started the engines. From every hatch and turret the crew were watching the other six aircraft for signs of trouble.

'You know, skipper,' drawled Merralls, the wireless

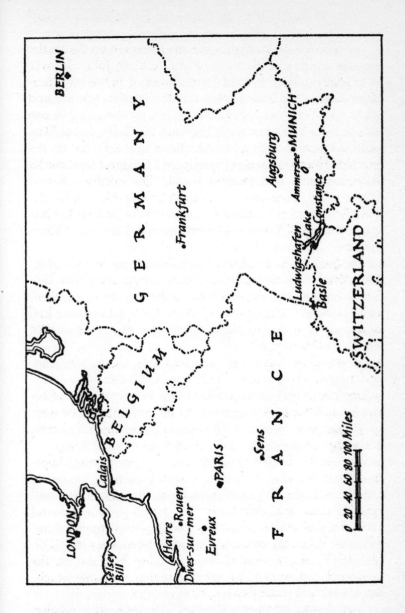

operator, 'I almost wish now we've got this far that we were going.'

The others quickly shouted him down. Then the flight engineer cut in.

'I don't like the look of "A for Apple",' he said. 'He's bashing No. 1 up and down a lot. I think he's got a mag. drop.'

It all looked different now. The crew fell silent. That slight feeling of detachment had evaporated.

' "A for Apple" has shut down,' said the flight engineer. So the reserve aircraft went in. Somehow they had all expected it.

Rodley thought of his wife back in Woodhall Spa. She would probably guess what had happened. He took off with the others and moved into the No. 3 position, tucked in to port of Sherwood. They rendezvoused with 44 Squadron at Selsey Bill.

It seemed to Sherwood that Nettleton was taking a course slightly north of their briefed track, and he checked with his navigator, who agreed. 'All right,' said Sherwood, 'we'll steer our own course. We're supposed to open up before we get to the target and bomb independently. It won't hurt to open up now.'

The two flights of six drew slowly apart. Several miles separated them as they approached the French coast west of Le Havre, with Nettleton's flight well to the north and still in the lead. It was a beautiful April day with no cloud, and most of the crews peeled off their tunics and loosened their ties. Each section of three kept tight formation, ready to bring the strongest possible combined fire-power to bear against enemy fighters.

Crossing the French coast the pilots had to climb to negotiate the cliffs and the sensation of speed was terrific. The peaceful French countryside with its many chateaux looked poignantly beautiful in the spring sunshine. But with a shattering roar and reverberation the twelve Lancasters plunged through it, clinging to the ground in tight, nerve-straining formation, following the earth's contours as closely as a trunk road. The pilots sat rigidly, in hypnotic concentration, watching the ground rush towards them in a great rolling torrent, looking up at the horizon, manipulating the throttles with one outstretched hand, easing the stick backwards and forwards with the other, tucking in close, following the leader, drawing a straight line across the earth's surface to Augsburg. Augsburg, Bavaria. Five hundred miles across Occupied Europe, into the heart of the German Reich. Augsburg, here we come.

Seven men in each Lancaster. Eight in the leading aircraft piloted by Nettleton. Eighty-five men. All determined to reach and hit their target. All hoping to get back.

Here at last in the Avro Lancaster, still on the secret list, was a weapon which might encompass the destruction of the industrial power behind Germany's military might. Thirty tons of aircraft, four engines racing, driving across France like a tank. Six of them, and then another six, their crews tense with the risk of collision, sweeping a path two hundred yards wide across Europe, closing on their target at the rate of three miles a minute.

Get down as low as you can, they had said. That's the way to avoid the fighters. That's the way to escape detection. Workers in the fields, their ear-drums assaulted with noise, hardly had time to look up before the twin-tail-units of the Lancasters dipped below the next hill.

The crews could see their upturned faces clearly. Everyone on the ground stopped what they were doing and gaped. The noise burst upon them with the suddenness of a bomb. But one old Frenchman saw them coming and just had time to sweep off his hat and make a cavalier bow before flattening himself against the road.

Nettleton and the leading six Lancasters were flying over a small wood when the first ground flak began to search for them. It could be no more than an isolated battery, probably using the camouflage of the wood, but the fire was accurate and two aircraft were hit. The only serious damage was sustained by Beckett; his rear turret was hit and put out of action. This would be a fatal handicap if they were attacked by fighters. But Beckett did not break formation and the section kept on in tight formation after Nettleton.

Accurate timing of the diversionary operation had been an essential of success. If the Bostons with their fighter support attacked too soon, the German fighters might be back at their bases in time to refuel and intercept the Lancasters. If the attack were not soon enough, fighters scrambled near the Augsburg route might run into the Lancasters on their way south. Either way, some small incident which delayed or protracted the operations of a single German fighter squadron could result in an interception, and defeat the whole object of the diversion. The original plan had been for the Bostons and their escorting fighters to start their attacks ten minutes before the Lancasters crossed the French coast. Further consideration suggested that this was not soon enough. Even with radar warning, German fighters scrambled farther afield might not be clear of the Lancaster area in time. The adjustment, to fifty minutes before the Lancasters crossed the coast, took into account that the escorting fighters could keep the diversion going for some time after the actual attack. But the pendulum had been swung too far. There was a further reappraisal, and in the event, the main attack was allowed to develop about thirty minutes before the Lancasters crossed the coast.

But two squadrons of German fighters, alerted to intercept the Bostons, were on their way back to their airfield at Evreux, on a course which would cross the Lancasters' track. They passed well ahead of Sherwood and his squadron, but there was a grave danger that they might spot the six Lancasters to the north led by Nettleton.

The two sections of this flight were about 400 yards apart, and it was the second section, led by Sandford, which first picked out a cluster of specks high in the sky which could only be German fighters. Crum and Beckett closed up on Sandford until the three aircraft were wing-tip to wing-tip,

24

squatting as near the ground as they dared. The crops in the fields were flattened by their slipstream they were so low.

There was still a good chance of avoiding detection by the high-flying German fighters. But Alan Dedman, Crum's navigator, looking across to the right, picked out a stray fighter, perhaps returning early, wheels down and on its final approach into Evreux aerodrome. Just before the pilot completed his landing he would be almost bound to see the Lancasters silhouetted against the sky.

Pointing the fighter out to his pilot, Dedman watched it unblinkingly as it sank gently towards the ground. But it never landed. Suddenly the pilot whipped his wheels up and began to climb.

For a short time he flew on a parallel course to the Lancasters. Could he possibly be merely going round again? Then he turned decisively towards them.

The German pilot gained height before diving down at the Lancasters. The crews of Sandford's section saw the red spots flash along the fighter's wing-tips as the tracers darted towards them. One bullet splashed through the canopy of Crum's aircraft and showered Crum and Dedman with splinters of perspex. Dedman watched the blood trickling down his pilot's face, but Crum gave a reassuring grin.

Suddenly the air around them was filled with milling, writhing, twisting black crosses as the high-flying pack of German fighters, warned from the ground, dived into the attack. There were thirty of them, in two formations of fifteen, Me 109s, and F.W. 190s intermingled, and a fierce running fight developed as the Lancaster gunners began to pick their targets. The combined fire-power of three Lancasters was something new to the German pilots, but they had the answer to it. They began their attack from the port quarter, closing from 700 yards to 400 and then breaking away. They had never seen a Lancaster before, but they knew that the British 0.303 machine-guns were ineffective above 400 yards. They kept at long range, outgunning the

Lancasters with their cannon. The tight formation of the Lancasters, instead of presenting the maximum defensive fire-power, only made a better target.

Still the Lancasters went roaring on over the countryside, lifting over the hills and skimming down the valleys, while fighter after fighter attacked from astern. The pilots could hear the racket of answering fire from their turrets and see the German cannon shells tearing up the ground ahead.

They rushed over the roofs of a village, watching cannon shells crashing ahead of them into houses, blowing holes in street walls and smashing into the gables of roofs. Again and again this second section was hit. If the Germans had the range to stay with them they must all be shot down.

Beckett was the first to go. His aircraft, with its rear turret out of action, had attracted the bulk of the attack from the first. Soon, a mass of flames from end to end, it began to drop back, and a moment later the gunners of the remaining aircraft saw it crash into a tree and disintegrate.

Now the pack turned its attention to Crum, converging in a wide arc from a dozen angles – from astern and from the flanks and diving down from above. The interior of the fuselage became a death-trap of ricocheting bullets. Both the mid-upper and rear gunners shouted that they were hit. Then a fire started in the port wing as Crum fought to keep control.

'Jettison the bombs!'

Crum's shouted signal was acted on immediately by Dedman, and the bombs, jettisoned 'safe', fell away. But the aircraft, shredded and bespattered like a towed target, still wallowed dangerously.

Crum was a wily bird, old in years and experience by comparison with most of the others, and although the temptation to pull the nose of the Lancaster up for safety was strong, he knew this was what the fighters were waiting for. Deciding that there was nothing left for him to do but fly the Lancaster into the ground wheels up as they had planned, and seeing a wheat-field dead ahead, he jerked the nose forward to escape another concerted fighter attack, shut the throttles, and at the last minute levelled off. The crew, convinced that he had lost control, braced themselves for a fatal crash.

Ploughing through the wheat like a huge harvester, the Lancaster came gently to rest at the edge of the field. Fear of fire was the spur as the crew fought their way out, but Dowty, the front gunner, was trapped in the nose turret. His belief that the bombs were still in the bomb-bay and that he had eleven seconds to live added a frantic urgency to his shouts for help. Crum attacked the turret with an axe and got him out.

The smooth surfaces of the Lancaster had been transformed into a jagged and splayed façade of torn metal. But the fire that had threatened in the air had petered out and the interior was still virtually intact. They had made the Germans a present of a brand new aircraft still on the secret list.

Perforating the petrol tanks with the axe, Crum tried to set fire to the escaping petrol by means of a Verey pistol. But it wouldn't ignite. Then someone threw a lighted match into the pool of petrol forming on the ground. The others backed away and shouted at him to stand clear, but instead of vanishing in the expected explosion they watched the petrol catch fire slowly at first and then more firmly. Soon the Lancaster was enveloped in flames.

Breaking up into small parties, they set out to walk to Unoccupied France. But they never reached the Black Cat Café at Bordeaux. In spite of courageous help from many Frenchmen, they were caught in the last stages of their journey to freedom.

Meanwhile Nick Sandford, the leader of the section, was facing the pack of German fighters alone. In desperation he forced his Lancaster down even lower, skimming over the ground at nought feet. Suddenly ahead of him he saw a line of telephone wires. He held the nose down and flew underneath them, hoping to catch his pursuers unawares; but they shot underneath the wires just behind him, firing all the way.

Sandford, a little fellow with a pleasing personality, was keen on music and bought all the records for the Officers' Mess. He always wore his pyjamas under his flying suit for luck. But this time he had no chance at all. With the fuselage riddled and all four engines ablaze, his aircraft crashed into the ground in an inferno of flame.

All this was described to the three pilots of the leading section over the inter-com by their gunners, who watched the destruction of Sandford's section in apprehensive horror. Now, as the whole pack chased after them, it was their turn. All the gunners opened up as the fighters bored in, but soon the defensive fire faltered as gun after gun started to jam.

Emboldened by lack of answering fire, one Me 109 pilot crept up behind Rhodes' aircraft, on the left of the formation, to within twenty-five yards, firing his cannon as he came. Flames and then more flames burst from all four engines of the Lancaster, streaking back beyond the tail-plane. Then this aircraft spurted forward like a whipped horse before climbing almost vertically, all engines burning, until it hovered directly above Nettleton and Garwell.

Inevitably the stall must come. And when it did, the crews of the other two Lancasters looked up to see an immense ball of flame diving straight at them.

The incident, enacted in a strangely protracted slow-motion, seemed to catch a moment of time and make it stand still. Miraculously the great diving inferno missed both aircraft by a few feet before plunging nose first into the ground, the whole fuselage seeming to compress and concertina on impact. Then there was nothing left except a great cloud of dust and smoke, and 'Dusty' Rhodes and his crew were gone.

That left only Nettleton and Garwell, and in a frenzy of aerobatic manoeuvring the fighters swept after them. Both aircraft were attacked repeatedly from the rear, blowing great holes in the fuselage and wing surfaces. Then a series of tell-tale puffs of vapour revealed that the petrol tanks in each aircraft had been holed.

An FW 190 pulled out of the pack and moved over to port, then wheeled round to come in from the beam. Stubby and tiny, its black crosses showing up plainly against its green-painted fuselage, it seemed, like some proud peacock, to display all the details of its silhouette before hurtling in for the kill. The crews could see the pilot sitting there, holding his fire. But a moment before he opened up, an accurate burst from Garwell's front gunner put him off his aim. He got in a hurried burst which went wide.

All this time neither Nettleton nor Garwell had attempted any evasive action, content to keep hugging the ground and rely on what defensive fire their gunners could put up. For any sort of evasive action they needed more height –and that would give the German pilots the opportunity to attack from below. But both men realised that their situation was hopeless. The self-sealing petrol tanks seemed to be working and there was now only an occasional puff of vapour, but all Nettleton's guns were out of action and Garwell had only two or three guns still firing. If the German fighters could stay with them, both aircraft were doomed. The carefully planned daylight raid on Augsburg would be cut to half-strength.

But now this tragic chance encounter ended. The German fighters, scrambled earlier to intercept the Bostons, had been airborne for a long time and they were running out of petrol. After a few more bursts of cannon they turned back to Evreux, convinced that the two remaining Lancasters couldn't get far.

Nettleton and Garwell still had nearly 500 miles to go to the target. Both were practically defenceless. The orders had been that if one aircraft of a section was shot down in the early stages of the flight, that section was to return. The squadron had lost four out of six. But Nettleton never considered going back, and neither did Garwell.

*       *       *

The 97 Squadron Lancasters, led by Sherwood, saw nothing of the fighters. Over to the north on the horizon they caught a glimpse of several aircraft crashing in flames. Some poor devils were catching it. That was all they thought about it. They never connected it with their own raid.

The whole defences of France and southern Germany were now alerted, and the remaining Lancasters could expect further opposition before they reached the target. But the stratagem of flying a route apparently aimed at Munich deceived the Germans completely. All flak-posts in the Munich area were alerted and fighters waited for them over the city in vain.

The remaining hours to the target were a succession of kaleidoscopic images rushing at them and away. First a parade-ground packed with German soldiers, a burst of machine-gun fire from a rear turret, and an empty parade ground.

Then glimpses of peaceful valleys untouched by war as the two formations forged ahead over mountainous country, while upward and downward air currents made formation flying more and more hazardous.

Then a frontier post on the Swiss-German border. An SS man in close-up – black uniform, black boots and black cap – shaking his fist at them, then running back down the road towards a telephone box as they disappeared from view. The Rhine, a beautiful, rolling river. Lake Constance, and a small white ferry-boat chugging across. A German officer, standing in the stern, points his Luger at them defiantly and fires. They can even see the smoke from the barrel.

Then Lake Ammer, the last turning point, ten miles south of the target, where an old bearded Bavarian, standing on the shores of the lake, takes pot shots at them with a duck-gun.

'Shall I tickle him up?' asks a gunner.

'No, leave him alone.'

Thus they crossed half Europe, Nettleton and Garwell out ahead, Sherwood and his formation still intact some miles behind. Reaching Lake Ammer, Nettleton and Garwell turned north for Augsburg.

There was no low cloud and they could see for twenty miles, but straight ahead the ground humped away from them, shutting, them off from their target. Nettleton pulled up gently to climb the hill, like a fast car in top gear, shot over the top, and there before them lay Augsburg.

It was a trim, peaceful-looking Bavarian town, about the size of Basingstoke. But before they reached the outskirts the flak began to rise at them.

The intention had been to fly straight from here to the target, but ahead Nettleton saw a bed of chimney-stacks which would force him to gain height. This, with the flak already thick and accurate from a flak-tower directly in front of him, he was determined not to do. He thought he could see a clearer run in from the east, so he turned to starboard, away from the flak-tower, crossed the Munich railway line, and kept going until he was level with the centre of the town. Then he saw what he was looking for – the line of the river. He turned back to port, pushed the nose of his Lancaster down still farther, and followed the river. Garwell kept with him and the two Lancasters burst like a tidal wave into the town.

Although they had studied the exact appearance of the target from photographs and models at briefing that morning, they were astonished now at their accuracy. They recognised the whole lay-out instantly, although they were approaching from an unexpected angle. Their primary target was not simply the works as a whole but one particular T-shaped shed where the submarine engines were made. There it was, directly ahead, perhaps a quarter of a mile distant, carefully camouflaged but unmistakable.

Low-angle flak was pouring at them in a continual stream, so low that the Germans were firing into their own buildings. Both aircraft were hit repeatedly.

'Bomb-doors open.'

The roof-tops of Augsburg flickered by beneath them like a fast-flowing river. A sandbagged gun-post on top of the main factory building was firing at them point-blank. The front-gunners fired back. Then the gun-post disappeared beneath the nose of the two Lancasters and the bomb-aimers pressed their release-buttons.

'Bombs gone.'

Nettleton swung his aircraft to port, taking the evasive action he had longed to take, and Garwell, his aircraft wallowing uncertainly, managed to follow. Then Nettleton turned back to starboard, heading west, and looked back over his shoulder at the target.

It was several seconds since they had dropped their load. Eight 1000-pound bombs would go up at any moment.

Everyone who could crane his neck to do so watched the T-shaped shed. There was a moment of distortion when the entire factory seemed to blur and become indistinct, and then whole sections of the shed and the surrounding buildings tumbled outwards or were blasted helplessly into the air.

At this point Garwell broke formation and began to gain height. 'Watch him!' yelled Nettleton to his gunners. 'See what happens to him.'

Nettleton kept on a rough westerly heading and Garwell followed some distance behind. Suddenly Garwell heard Flux, his wireless operator, yelling in his ear.

'We're on fire!'

Flux kept pointing over his shoulder, and Garwell took a quick look behind him. The armour-plated door leading into the fuselage was open and the interior was a mass of flames. This was a fire which would never be put out.

'Shut the door!' ordered Garwell. He decided to crash-land at once rather than attempt to climb and bale out. The quicker they were on the ground the better. Five of the crew had crowded into the front cockpit but there were still two men behind that wall of fire.

Garwell could see Nettleton and some of his crew staring at the burning Lancaster and he gave them an impolite version of the V-sign, which they instantly returned. Then he turned to port into wind and made for a patchwork of fields south of the town.

As he throttled back and lowered the flaps, smoke started to pour into the cabin, blinding him so that he couldn't see out or read the instruments, and choking him so that he could hardly breathe. All five men in the front cabin were coughing violently, and Flux opened the escape hatch over the navigator's table to try to get some air.

Garwell kept the aircraft going at what he thought was the same angle, and then a sudden down-draught from the hatch cleared the smoke for a fraction of a second and he saw a line of tall trees straight ahead of them, blocking their path. He opened up the engines and pulled back on the stick, but already the smoke had closed in again.

He must have cleared the trees by now. He throttled back again and pushed the nose gently forward. He could not see anything. He was flying her into the ground blind at eighty miles an hour. All he could do was hold off and hope. But when the impact came she settled down like an old hen, sliding on her belly for about fifty yards and then stopping gently. They made a dash for the hatch.

Outside they found Flux lying dead under the starboard inner engine. He had been thrown out on impact. His quick action in opening the hatch had probably saved their lives. The whole body of the aircraft was burning furiously and they couldn't get near the two men in the fuselage.

Nettleton, alone of his formation, set course for home. He and Garwell had dropped their bombs accurately and done considerable damage, but two aircraft could not do the work of six. The success of the raid now depended on Sherwood and the crews of the second flight.

The leading section, Sherwood, Rodley and Hallows, were just topping the rise of the hill overlooking Augsburg as Nettleton disappeared into the setting sun. Rodley, the most youthful in appearance, with a whimsical sense of humour, was the oldest at twenty-eight. A genuine precision flyer, he was later to become a Boeing 707 pilot with BOAC. 'Darky'

Hallows, so called because of his black hair and black moustache, was the squadron character, whose R/T phraseology after a sticky trip was so colourful that WAAF operators were hurriedly shepherded away when he came in to land. He had resigned a commission in the King's Liverpool Regiment to join the RAF.

As the three aircraft cleared the hill their crews could see two columns of black smoke in the centre of the town and they knew that 44 Squadron had delivered their attack and that the defences would be fully alerted. This was confirmed as the flak-tower south of the town began to get their range. Every gun in the town was firing at them and Sherwood decided to go straight in. There was no time for a detour and he pulled up to 300 feet to clear the chimney stacks on the run in to the target.

He pushed his throttles forward and Rodley and Hallows opened up to keep station. The formation speeded up to close on 240 miles an hour, bunched in tight because the target was narrow and all three aircraft must bomb simultaneously. To go in one by one would give the defences the chance to concentrate their fire on one aircraft.

The Germans began to hose their tracer across the spread of the formation and the crews could hear it banging against the metal surfaces of their aircraft, like handfuls of gravel on a corrugated iron roof. All they could do was fly through it. Sherwood, in the centre, was forced to hold steady, but Rodley and Hallows weaved very slightly in pitch, presenting as difficult a target as possible.

The nearer they got to the factory the thicker flowed the flak. Whole chunks of buildings were dislodged and broke into fragments beneath them as the German 88-millimetre shells crashed through. They had been told that most of the flak defences were heavy stuff which couldn't get down to their height, but the air was filled with ugly black smudges that could only be heavy ack-ack. One of these heavy shells hit Hallows' aircraft in the starboard wing and the whole aircraft shuddered. Miraculously it passed between the main

34

wing tank and the aileron control without exploding and kept going. Cutting, the bomb-aimer, stretched out in the nose to drop his bombs, with his head stuck between the front gunner's legs, felt the blow. 'We've been hit!' he shouted, 'this kite's shaking like a leaf!' 'Shut up,' returned the gunner, 'that's my knees.'

They were making their attack straight into the front of the factory, aiming at the main gate, like a film camera panning through the entrance to a castle. So absorbed were the crews in their flying and bombing and gunnery problems that for a moment fear was forgotten. The strain on the pilots was terrific as they strove to hold formation, keeping a lookout ahead for obstructions and trying to follow their bomb-aimer's orders to line up on the target.

Sherwood was aiming for the centre of the diesel-engine shop. The bomb-aimers in the two outside aircraft urged their pilots to get over, the one to the left, the other to the right. But the leading aircraft was in the way. Each pilot dropped back a little and pulled in slightly behind Sherwood, riding his slipstream, so as to give his bomb-aimer a better chance.

A quarter of a mile from the target they selected bomb-doors open. The machine-gun post on the top of the factory was pouring tracer at them. There was no weaving now, just a wild scramble for position, like horses bunched together before a jump. The front gunners sprayed back at the machine-gun post, the mid-upper and rear gunners opened up at any other sites they could see. All the gunners shouted wildly and excitedly as they worked their turrets, exulting in the chance to hit back.

Four successive lurches in each aircraft told that the thousand-pounders had gone. Each pilot snapped his bomb-doors closed immediately for greater protection. There were no large buildings or chimneys ahead and Sherwood pushed his aircraft right down almost to street level, escaping most of the flak. Rodley and Hallows followed. Now even the houses gave them shelter.

The defensive fire began to thin out a little, but there was one persistent gunner who refused to give up. They had reached the outskirts of the town but someone was throwing huge tracer shells after them, horribly close. The shells bounced on the ground around them and ricocheted into the air, racing past them, first to port and then to starboard. 'If this chap's not careful,' thought Rodley, 'he's going to hit me.' Just then he noticed a puff of white vapour streak back from Sherwood's aircraft. It looked like glycol. They must have been hit in an engine.

Quickly the tiny puff grew into a stream of white vapour. Rodley and Hallows could see that a petrol tank had been holed. Sherwood was losing petrol fast. Rodley went to flick his microphone on to warn him – breaking R/T silence couldn't matter now – but before he could do so the stream of vapour had thickened and turned black. Sherwood's aircraft was on fire.

Still Sherwood kept going, and still from force of discipline the other two formated on him. Sherwood got lower and lower but Rodley and Hallows stayed with him, hypnotised by his nearness, feeling that some taint of disloyalty was involved in turning away. They could see Sherwood clearly, his navigator standing next to him, flames already licking into the cockpit. Then at last the aircraft began to slip underneath them, and looking down they saw that the hatch at the top of the fuselage had burned away and that the inside was a roaring tunnel of fire. Outside there was still nothing visible except the plume of black smoke. Then gradually the aircraft dropped back.

'Keep an eye on them,' called Rodley to his gunners. 'See if anyone gets out.'

The burning Lancaster was now out of control, and a moment later it tore into the earth at full flying speed and exploded into a chrysanthemum of flame. 'Oh Christ, skipper,' shouted the rear gunner. There was no chance for anyone in there.

The two surviving Lancasters, both severely damaged,

turned for home, clinging to each other for support and strength until dark.

Now it was the turn of the last section.

Led by Flight Lieutenant Penman, with Flying Officer Deverill No. 2 and Warrant Officer Mycock No. 3, this section had circled for three minutes north of the Ammer See to give Sherwood's section time to get clear. Penman was a square, chunky Scot, like Sherwood only twenty-three. Deverill was twenty-six, an ex-apprentice with eleven years' service, recently commissioned and a veteran of over a hundred operational flights. He already had the DFM. Mycock, slight and ginger-haired, had won the DFC in a daylight raid on the *Scharnhorst* and *Gneisenau* in Brest.

As these three pilots began their final run up to the target they saw Sherwood crash. Then they flew into the biggest barrage of all. The German gunners had now perfected their technique of lobbing heavy stuff from a distance, and the light flak was more concentrated than ever. In spite of accurate return fire from the air gunners, all the flak posts – even the one on the roof of the factory – were still firing.

The crews of both squadrons had acquired their own private sheets of armour plating, and had them fitted where they felt most vulnerable. For the men of the last three Lancasters there was nothing to do now but crouch into position at battle stations and wait.

About a mile from the target Penman and Deverill were aware of a bright glow in the sky. The wireless-operators, immured in the darkened fuselage, were even more conscious of it. They rushed to the nearest hatch and peered out.

Mycock's aircraft, still in tight formation, was a flying sheet of flame. The whole port wing was ablaze, throwing a bright orange incandescence across the sky.

Heartened by their success, the German gunners poured a wall of flak into the whole section. Deverill's aircraft was the next to be hit. 'We're on fire!' shouted the mid-upper gunner. Clouds of smoke and flame were choking him in the fuselage. 'Put it out, then,' yelled ex-apprentice Deverill, 'I've got enough to do up here.' The starboard inner engine was pouring smoke and flame and he was fighting to hold his position.

Crippled as their aircraft were, in imminent danger of exploding, neither Deverill nor Mycock deviated from his bombing course. The three Lancasters charged on for the target in an arrow of flame.

Irons, Deverill's wireless operator, left his set to help put out the fire. The oil recuperators had been punctured and burning oil was trickling down the fuselage into the well of the aircraft. While the crews of these two aircraft fought the fire, fought indeed for their lives, the men up front ignored their peril and concentrated on flying the aircraft and hitting the target and pouring machine-gun fire into the German flak-posts.

In the last quarter of a mile to the target Mycock's aircraft became almost completely enveloped in flames. The other crews saw the pilot's window open, but Mycock made no sign. They saw his bombs fall on the factory. Then his aircraft blew up.

Mycock had been hit at the beginning of the run up and he could have pulled away to force-land or pulled up to bale out at any time in the last two miles. He preferred to hold his course and drop his bombs before considering personal safety. By then it was too late.

Mycock's navigator was an old school friend from his home town. They had been overjoyed to get crewed up together. His second pilot had refused to take third light on a match from Irons that morning. 'Not now, Ron,' he had said. 'Tonight perhaps I will.' Irons had taken it himself.

Deverill's aircraft left the target on three engines and with the fourth still ablaze. The fuselage was blackened and gutted and ten feet of the plating on one side had burnt completely away, but the frantic efforts of the crew eventually got the fire under control. MacKay, the mid-upper gunner, who had been growing a moustache to go on leave with and had just reached the stage of twiddling the ends, had one half singed off in the fire and had to shave the other half when he got back.

The Germans claimed to have shot this aircraft down, and Penman's crew, too, were certain it had been lost. One of Penman's gunners found tears streaming down his face at the sight of them on fire, and the whole of Penman's crew shouted their heads off when Deverill formated on them later, the fire extinguished. Deverill had pushed the throttles wide open to catch up with Penman as all his turrets were jammed, but how much help Penman could have given them he learnt when they got back. 'Lucky for us you turned up,' said Penman, 'all our guns were out.'

The last view these two crews had of the factory was of a smouldering wreck, the flak-post on the roof-top silenced at last.

All the way home the crews expected retribution from German fighters, such was the respect in which the Germans were held at that time. But once over the Channel they relaxed, spat out the wads of gum that they'd been chewing since take-off, had a coffee, congratulated each other on getting away with it, and talked of the chances of the missing crews. Usually one could find a grain of hope, but for Sherwood and Mycock and their crews, and three of the four shot down by the fighters on the way out, there was none. Someone would have the task of telling the wives. Most of them lived out near the bases.

In spite of their heavy losses it was a triumphant return. The planners had been optimistic but the squadrons hadn't expected to see them again and they were given an emotional greeting. Then someone handed each man a cup of coffee laced with rum and they sat down in the briefing room to shoot their lines.

Afterwards Penman went to see Sherwood's wife, intent on breaking the news to her gently but realising that he could hold out no hope. He told her that he had seen him go in, that the aircraft had blown up. She shook her head. 'I would have known if he'd died,' she said. So many wives said this.

'I'm convinced he's all right. Don't worry.' To Penman this was infinitely worse than a flood of tears, but he supposed it would soon sink in, and then would come the reaction.

Some time later came the news that all but three of Garwell's crew had survived; and then, after six weeks, came the astonishing tidings that Sherwood was alive. His survival had been a miracle. When the blazing aircraft hit the deck it had disintegrated, but Sherwood, strapped into his heavily armour-plated seat, had been catapulted through the canopy of the Lancaster and his fall had been broken by trees. He had suffered no more than minor burns. All his crew were killed.

Photographs taken a few days after the raid revealed extensive damage to the factory, concentrated in the vital diesel assembly shop and test bench. Production was not completely stopped but work was delayed and the factory was not back to normal for six months.

'Undeterred by heavy losses at the outset,' wrote Churchill, '44 and 97 pierced in broad daylight into the heart of Germany and struck a vital point with deadly precision. We must plainly regard the attack as an outstanding achievement.' 'Bomber' Harris for once was even more eloquent. 'The gallant adventure penetrating deep into the heart of Germany in daylight and pressed with outstanding determination in the face of bitter and foreseen opposition,' he signalled to the two squadrons, 'takes its place among the most courageous operations of the war.' Harris had held out high hopes that the raid would become a pattern for others but he now realised that heavier calibre armament would be needed to take on German fighters in daylight, even in the new Lancaster. This would counter the enemy tactics of employing their cannon from outside the effective range of the bombers' machine-guns. Another recommendation was that a suitable delay fuse of about half an hour was wanted to enable aircraft to break formation near the target and attack from different directions, thus confusing ground defences and preventing all guns from being lined up on one line of approach.

The diversionary operations had not succeeded in engaging sufficient enemy fighters in combat, and as a result a third of the Lancaster force had been lost at the start. But this was a fault that might be corrected for any future attack. And although it had been intended that the two squadrons should give each other mutual support against fighters, it did not seem likely that the losses would have been much different had they stayed together. More significant were the losses over the target – three aircraft out of eight, and a fourth aircraft – Deverill's – a complete write-off. Successful as the raid had been in that it had achieved its immediate object, the cost had been too great. Nothing like it was ever attempted again until the German defences were collapsing in 1945.

The last congratulations came several days later from Sir Dudley Pound, the Chief of Naval Staff. Quite properly he had waited for confirmation. 'I have now seen the photographs and assessment,' he wrote. 'I am sure this attack will have greatly helped in achieving our object. I much deplore the comparatively heavy casualties but I feel sure their loss was not in vain.'

This considered view by the Chief of Naval Staff was later challenged by the Ministry of Economic Warfare, who, put out of countenance because Harris had not consulted them on the choice of target, quickly suggested two other targets which they felt might have been more profitable and more worthy of sacrifice. Backed by the Prime Minister, Harris easily demolished their objections. But the question remained – was it worth it? 'Absolutely,' answered Nettleton. He had not forgotten his former comrades the merchant seamen, nor the effect, however difficult to assess, that the raid must have on the U-Boat war. But even more than these things he was proud of having helped to demonstrate that in the midst of the crushing defeats of early 1942 the offensive spirit was still alive in Britain.

Of the eighty-five men who set out for Augsburg on that

April afternoon, forty-nine were missing. Of the remainder, only a handful survived the war.

Early in 1943 Nettleton, who was awarded the VC for this raid, was given command of a squadron and promoted to wing commander. He was killed in action over Turin on 12 July 1943. His epitaph, which can stand for all the 55,000 men of Bomber Command who lost their lives, can best be given in his own words. *'The war can't be finished,'* he said in a broadcast after the Augsburg raid, *'without attacking the enemy.'*

Surely there are few attacks in the history of air warfare which were pressed home by crew after crew with such valour.

# 2

## The Highlander

'I'M BROWNED OFF,' wrote LAC George Thompson, 22-year-old son of a Kinross ploughman, seizing the chance of a short break in his ground wireless duties to write a letter home. It was 1 January 1943, and he thought he had never spent a duller New Year's Day. 'It's not that I want to do any of that heroic stuff,' he went on, 'but this job isn't very exciting.'

Twelve months' overseas service in Iraq, Persia and the Persian Gulf had not satisfied George Thompson's desire for adventure, and soon after writing this letter he applied for a transfer to flying duties. Two years later, on another New Year's Day, 'that heroic stuff' was to win him the award of the VC.

Thompson had left school at fourteen to become a grocer's assistant, and had later qualified as a certificated grocer. Tall, big-boned, and immensely strong, he had a brusque downrightness of speech which was accentuated by a strong Scots accent; but his rugged exterior was softened by the gentle manner of the typical Highlander. Quiet, obliging, and conscientious, he was a youth who saw nothing menial in the service of his fellow men. Serving in the shop at Kinross, or driving the delivery van to outlying farms, he was always ready to help others. As a boy he had loved tinkering with wireless sets, and many a time on his rounds he traced and repaired some minor fault for a lonely couple whose radio was their only contact with the outside world. He ran their errands for them, filled in their ration books, posted their letters, and took their wireless batteries into Kinross to be charged. He was the perfect errand boy.

43

Thompson's application for aircrew training was successful, and in the late autumn of 1944 he reported for duty with his crew at No. 9 Squadron, Bardney, Lincolnshire. His pilot was a twenty-five-year-old farmer from New Zealand, Harry Denton, quiet and shy, studious and teetotal, not a good mixer socially, but keen on a good crew spirit. On arrival at their operational training unit Denton, looking around for a likely crew, had picked out Ron Goebel, a tall, fair, pale young man who had trained as a navigator and then been transferred to bomb-aiming because of a shortage. Denton found Goebel keen and surprisingly mature for his age, and the two men agreed to join forces. Like Denton, Goebel drank little and did not smoke, and took life fairly seriously without being devoid of a sense of humour.

Next Denton was introduced to a navigator named Ted Kneebone, an NCO from Manchester, slightly built and alert, neat and quick in his movements and at his work. It was Kneebone who picked out George Thompson, impressed at once by the steady brown eyes and open face and pleasant Scots burr. The two men became firm friends and went everywhere together. Kneebone found Thompson, although outwardly the strong, silent type, thoroughly articulate on subjects which interested him, and fanatically proud of his Scots ancestry, which he was always prepared to defend in argument, if necessary with his fists. He was no prude, and liked his pint of beer, but he had a deep religious sense, and the two men frequently went to Evensong together on a Sunday, calling in afterwards at a local pub to listen to the talk of the country folk.

It was Kneebone, too, who picked the two Welsh gunners, Haydn Price, short and thick-set, with a slow, friendly smile, and Ernie Potts, oldest man in the crew, married and exempt from war service because of his work as an agricultural engineer, until he chose to volunteer. Like Thompson he had begun on ground duties and then applied for a transfer to air crew. Two months earlier his wife had presented him with a daughter, Christine, and the whole crew planned to go to Newport on their next leave to wet the baby's head.

Both Price and Potts, true to Welsh tradition, loved singing, and the inter-com was often loaded with Welsh melodies – until someone shut them up. Many, too, were the bantering arguments between Scots and Welsh, with New Zealand, the North Country, and the South chipping in. Like most bomber crews they became a composite, revelling in their differences and in their mutual confidence.

And so to New Year's Eve 1945, and the rhythmic thump of 'Paper Doll' escaping into the crisp night air from the All Ranks dance at the blacked-out Naafi. Inside, the atmosphere was smoky but electric. Hundreds of young people jostled on the tiny floor or fought for drinks at the inadequate bar. With victory almost in sight after more than five years, there had never been so exciting a prospect as the New Year of 1945. Then the Tannoy blared. 'Attention please. Attention please. The following pilots will report to the Operations Room. . . .'

The orchestra faded out unevenly. The girls who were dancing with flying men clutched the lapels of their jackets. Germany wasn't beaten yet. For ten Lancaster crews the party, perhaps 1945 itself, was over.

The take-off was timed for just before dawn. That meant an early call at 5 am. The band started again and the party went on, more fiercely than ever now, but for seventy men of the Lancasters the night had gone sour. No sense in flying on a daylight raid without a clear head. One by one they slipped away to bed.

Around five o'clock next morning the fierce jet of an electric torch shone full in the face by the duty crew woke even the heaviest sleepers, and after a hurried breakfast the crews reported to briefing. It was freezing hard and the briefing hut was white with frost. There they learned their target – the Dortmund–Ems Canal. They picked up their flying clothing from their lockers in the crew room and drove out to dispersal. All ten Lancasters, too, were white with hoarfrost. The crews piled into their aircraft, seeking warmth.

Because of frost and fog few of them had flown in the past fortnight, and the seats and controls had a moment's unfamiliarity for each of them. Then they settled in and were at home again.

Before turning on to the runway, each aircraft was sprayed with glycol to remove the rime, and with glycol still dripping from the wings Denton turned his Lancaster into wind and roared down the runway as the first aircraft off. Ted Kneebone, the navigator, sat watching the airspeed indicator, calling out the speeds to the pilot : 100 . . . 110 . . . 120 . . . 130 . . . At 140 she should come unstuck. But at 145 they were still roaring along the runway. And at 150 he couldn't keep the urgency out of his voice. They were running out of runway. Then at last she came off.

Whether it was ice still unmelted on the wings, the lack of wind, or carburettor icing, is uncertain, but the second aircraft had the same trouble. It crashed at the end of the runway and burst into flames. A third aircraft had the same experience and crashed but the crew escaped. A fine start to New Year's Day.

Three hours later the remaining crews, with ninety more from other squadrons, were nearing the target. Ten thousand feet below them, crystal clear in the frosty air, lay the great man-made waterways of North-West Germany, especially important to the Germans now that their railways had been bombed into chaos. And in the distance, running obliquely across their track, lay the greatest of them all, the Dortmund–Ems Canal.

Kneebone sat now in the nose compartment searching for his pinpoint, the River Glane at Ladbergen. Here, where an aqueduct carried the waters of the canal over the river, was a target especially vulnerable to bombing, and twice in the previous three months it had been seriously breached. But with ant-like persistence the Germans had repaired it, and now the canal was full again, ready to carry its traffic of coal and raw materials to the factories of the Ruhr.

The target identified, Denton settled down on his bombing run. Ron Goebel crouched at his bomb sight in the bombing compartment, calling instructions to Denton on the intercom.

'Three degrees starboard.'

It was impossible for Denton to make much use of such small corrections for evasive action, and the flak was thickening. The run up to the target was so good that most of the time Goebel used only a single word : 'Steady.'

That was easy to say, thought Denton, as he watched several of the aircraft ahead of him suffering direct hits from the murderous barrage of flak that was now pouring upwards from the banks of the canal as though some hidden ammunition dump had already been breached. Black puffs of smoke from 88 mm. shells darkened the sky. Heading into a 100-mph gale as they were, the bombing run seemed interminable.

At last the crew felt a slight bump as the first thousand-pounder left the bomb-bay, followed in quick succession by eleven more as the rest of the stick of twelve, spaced twelve yards apart, fell away. Denton pushed forward hard on the control column, correcting the tendency to climb as the load changed.

In a moment Goebel would have completed his check that all the bombs were safely away. Then he would give the signal 'Bombs gone', and Denton would close the bomb-doors, re-trim the aircraft, and turn away from the target area. Kneebone was back at the navigation table, working out the course to steer for home, waiting like Denton for the signal from Goebel. But it never came. Instead came the stupefying concussion and chaos from a direct hit by a salvo of two 88 mm. shells.

The first shell blew a gaping hole five or six feet square in the floor of the fuselage, just forward of the mid-upper turret, and set fire to the whole rear section of the aircraft. The front cockpit filled instantly with smoke, the rear fuselage was a sea of flames. Then, almost instantaneously, after the left to the solar plexus, came the knock-out right to the jaw – a second hit by heavy flak which shattered the nose compartment, set fire to an engine, and blew large holes in the pilot's canopy. Denton pitched forward unconscious and the aircraft dived out of control.

The explosive force of a 200-mph gale ripping through the shattered nose and canopy cleared the smoke in the cockpit and blew out the many candles of flame in the fuselage almost in one. Kneebone, in the navigator's seat behind the pilot, was sitting in a sea of flame one minute and in an Arctic gale the next. But a few flickers of flame from burning hydraulic oil around the damaged turrets survived and gained a hold.

Denton, blasted back to consciousness by the icy wind, surveyed a scene of appalling devastation. He was flying into the teeth of the gale as unprotected as in an aerial chair at a fairground. All his trimming knobs hung slack and useless, the hydraulics were gone, the bomb-doors were still open, the port inner engine was on fire, the inter-com was dead. The Lancaster had lost several thousand feet. And unknown to Denton there was the gaping hole in the fuselage, almost immediately above which sat the mid-upper gunner, trapped in his blazing turret. The rear turret too was on fire and the gunner trapped.

Thompson, sitting in the wireless seat to the rear of the forward compartment, had been the nearest of the men up front to the first explosion, and he knew that the rear fuselage must have been badly hit. He feared at once for the safety of the two gunners, Ernie Potts in the mid-upper turret, and Haydn Price in the rear.

The wireless seat was the warmest in the plane, and Thompson was not wearing gloves, which in any case would have impeded his operation of the morse key. He was not wearing a parachute either – the wireless operator's parachute was normally stowed beside him in the fuselage. But when the smoke and dust cleared and he peered down the fuselage and caught a brief glimpse of Potts slumped in his blazing turret, he made his way aft at once towards the gaping hole and the fire. There was no time to clip on his parachute or to search for gloves to protect his hands. Potts was in imminent danger of being badly burned or of struggling in a semi-conscious state out of his turret and falling to his death.

Meanwhile, miraculously enough, Denton had found that all the essential instruments seemed to be working and the aircraft still answered to the controls. He feathered the damaged engine and pressed the fire-extinguisher button and the fire stopped.

Goebel came up from the bombing compartment, carrying shreds of his parachute. Another parachute in the fuselage was on fire. With at least two of the crew unable to jump, it was no good giving the order to bale out.

With frozen fingers that were already being attacked by frostbite, Denton set a rough course that would take them back towards friendly territory – if the aircraft kept going. He called to Goebel. 'See if you can find me a pair of gloves, will you?' But Goebel couldn't hear. Eventually Denton made himself understood by dumb show, and Goebel went back into the fuselage.

He found Kneebone still at his seat, his face blackened with smoke. All his maps and charts had been sucked out of the aircraft, but he was working out a fresh course for Holland that would take them clear of the flak batteries of the bigger German towns. Hartshorn, the flight engineer, was with him. The wireless operator's seat immediately behind Kneebone was empty and there was no sign of Thompson. Goebel assumed that he had gone aft.

Rummaging about in the windswept fuselage, Goebel found a pair of gloves and then went forward to report to Denton. The rush of air was so great that he had to hold on with both hands to avoid being blown off his feet. He bent down to shout into Denton's ear, but the roar of three motors at full power drowned all other sound.

With the aircraft still trimmed tail-heavy for the bombing run and with no means of righting it, Denton sat rigidly with his shoulders braced against the backrest of his seat, pushing forward on the control column with all his strength to counteract the nose-up tendency and prevent the aircraft from stalling. At the same time he had to apply hard right rudder to balance the uneven pull of three engines.

The gaping hole in the floor of the fuselage, and the fire round both turrets, were still unknown to Denton or Goebel or any of the others in the front. They took the explosions of ammunition which they heard periodically to be answering fire from their own turrets, and assumed that they must be under fighter attack. They had too much to contend with up front to worry much about the rear. But Thompson knew what was happening in the rear. He had already made the safety of the two men there his personal responsibility.

The rescue of Potts was his first task. But to reach Potts involved the perilous passage past the gap in the floor of the fuselage. Looking for handholes and footholds in the side of the fuselage, moving with the careful deliberation of the rock climber, he clung to the side of the fuselage and inched his way aft until he was directly over the hole. There would be no chance for him if he fell.

Immediately aft of the hole was the mid-upper turret, flames licking up underneath it like a cauldron. One more grab at the protruding stanchion of metal, one more foothold in the ribbing of the fuselage shell, and he jumped down beyond the hole. Almost at once he was enveloped in flames.

Ammunition was exploding all round him. His clothes were alight but he ignored them. Holding on for a moment to the hot metal of the burning turret, he leaned out over the edge of the hole to force his shoulders under the dead weight of Potts' body before trying to lift him clear. Potts' clothes, too, were alight. He was unconscious.

Slowly Thompson dragged the gunner's arms and legs clear of the turret controls and manoeuvred his right shoulder until he could hunch it into Potts' midriff to take his weight. When he looked down he stared straight past the jagged edge of the broken fuselage at a drop of 6000 feet.

Working as rapidly as possible because of the flames licking around him, and yet at certain moments with ponderous deliberation in case he fell, he finally freed Potts from all encumbrances in the turret and felt the gunner's weight coming on to his shoulder. The next seconds would be critical.

The icy gale blowing through the fuselage helped to steady him and prevent him stumbling forward. But one downward lurch, such as the aircraft had already suffered when Denton collapsed over the controls, would precipitate both men into space.

Potts was now suspended over his shoulder, head and legs dangling. Thompson steadied him as best he could with one hand, but he needed the other to transfer his hold from the turret to the fuselage wall for balance. If Potts' body was not evenly distributed across his shoulders, or if he staggered for a moment under the gunner's weight, either or both of them would slip forward through the hole. But his strength and sense of balance did not fail him. Soon he was able to swing Potts round to the back of the turret, clear of the hole and the fire. He laid Potts down carefully, and at once began to beat out the flames in the gunner's clothes with his bare hands.

Thompson's trousers had been almost completely burned off and his legs had suffered. His face and hands too were severely burned. But he bent down again and lifted Potts to a safer resting-place. Then he looked aft again, through the flames surrounding the rear turret. Haydn Price, the other Welsh gunner, was still there.

All this time Thompson had been working alone. He had gone aft immediately after the explosion, and beyond the fact that some severe damage had been sustained in the nose of the aircraft as well, he had no idea what was happening up front. For all he knew, the order to bale out might have been given. The rest of the crew might have already gone. But he turned his back on the front of the aircraft and made his way aft to Price in the rear turret.

When the aircraft was first hit and the inter-com went dead Price had quickly realised that the fuselage was on fire. Cut off from the rest of the crew, he decided to bale out. The hydraulics were punctured, but in emergency the turret could be operated manually. All he had to do was turn the turret to one side and open the sliding door behind him, remove his helmet and the connections to his electrically-heated suit, and fall out backwards into space. All this took some time but at length he had manoeuvred the turret into position, released all the connections, and grasped his parachute release. Then he opened the sliding door. Immediately there was a tremendous blow-back of flames from outside the aircraft. The whole rear fuselage was trailing smoke and fire. In the few seconds in which he had the sliding door open, all his hair was singed off and both ears were severely burned. He slammed the door shut again, but the heat in the turret was becoming extreme, and he knew that the fire round the turret inside the fuselage was equally fierce. He had no alternative but to bale out even though it meant dropping backwards through the flames. He bent down to draw back the sliding door again. He didn't know that his seat-type parachute was already blackened and burned, and that if he baled out there was little chance that it would function properly.

As he grabbed the sliding door he heard a tapping from inside the fuselage. Incredibly, there must be someone there. He manoeuvred the turret back into the fore and aft position and drew back the sliding door.

'Come on, Taff,' said a voice, 'you'd better come out of there.' He would never have known it was Thompson if he hadn't recognised the voice.

Standing once again among the flames, Thompson half-dragged, half-carried Price clear of the turret and set him down next to Potts. Then he helped him beat out his burning clothing.

Still Thompson felt that his duty was not done. Somehow he must get through to the men up front to tell them of the state of the two gunners, lest the order be given to abandon the aircraft. Their only chance lay in a crash-landing. For the second time he began the perilous climb past the hole. It was doubly difficult now because of his burned hands and legs. His fingers too were frost bitten. Hunched against the fuselage wall, progressing painfully slowly in the teeth of the gale, he clung on as much with his elbows and knees and body as with his hands. Several times he was forced to stop altogether, flattened against the framework of the fuselage. Not until he was well past the hole did he dare to drop down to the fuselage floor, in case he was blown backwards as he did so. Then, the hole at last negotiated, he stumbled forward and shouted to the men in front that Potts and Price lay incapacitated in the rear.

Appalled at Thompson's condition, Kneebone and Hartshorn protected him from further exposure to the icy wind as best they could. Meanwhile Denton was still struggling to keep the Lancaster going until they reached the Allied lines. Approaching the Rhine they were down to 5000 feet.

Goebel, standing next to Denton on the look-out, pointed to a rash of anti-aircraft fire on the starboard side, and Denton immediately took evasive action. But almost at once the starboard inner motor failed. They had been hit again.

They began to lose height rapidly. Then, to the south of Arnhem, three FW 190s appeared out of the mist, flying straight at them. Fortunately the German fighters didn't stop. A Canadian Spitfire squadron was after them. Seeing the damaged Lancaster struggling home on two engines the Spitfire pilots broke off the engagement and escorted the bomber in, flying alongside at first, then opening up and slipping on ahead to lead it into the Spitfire base. But the Lancaster was almost finished now. Denton, still coaxing it along, pulling back on the stick, frozen stiff by the icy gale, was in a state of exhaustion. He knew that he had no more than a minute or so in which to put the plane down, and he looked around for a likely field.

Suddenly one of the Spitfire pilots swooped down in front

of the Lancaster and pulled up steeply before some apparent obstruction dead ahead, evidently as some kind of warning. Then Denton saw the danger. The crippled Lancaster was flying straight for a line of high-tension cables. With the last of his strength he dragged back on the control column and the Lancaster staggered clear.

Turning to avoid a village, Denton made for a patchwork of fields to his left. None of the fields looked much larger than a paddock. Denton chose two fields with a hedge between them and aimed the Lancaster diagonally across the two.

Crashing into the ground in the middle of the first field, the Lancaster ploughed through the hedge and the ridge of earth on which it stood, smashing what remained of the nose and breaking in two where the fuselage was weakened by the hole. Petrol poured from broken fuel pipes but somehow didn't catch fire.

Denton hit his head against the control column as they landed, but managed to climb clear. He then saw for the first time the damage to the fuselage. All the other crew members were able to stagger out, including Potts, who had recovered consciousness.

Thompson was the first man Denton saw. So pitiable was his condition that Denton didn't recognise him. His hands and face were blackened and his clothes were in shreds. But Thompson had no thought for his own injuries and was calling for help for Potts and Price. He called cheerily to Denton : 'Good landing, skipper !'

Goebel went off to get help while Denton, Kneebone and Hartshorn made for a nearby cottage, taking the injured men with them. It was obvious that Potts and Thompson were in bad shape, and Denton gave them both an injection of morphia. The little Dutch cottage filled with sympathetic villagers. Seeing the pathetic state of Potts and Thompson, most of the women wept.

The Spitfires had reported the Lancaster's position, and an ambulance with two doctors arrived within a few minutes. They were taken to a hospital in Eindhoven. Potts quickly lapsed into unconsciousness again, and died next day. All that Thompson had done for him had been in vain. His wife would become one of the many war widows who sacrificed everything to bring up and educate their fatherless children. Price was badly burned about the head, but was well enough to be flown home to hospital in England ten days later, where he recovered. Goebel was badly frost-bitten and lost all the top finger-joints of one hand, but he too made an otherwise full recovery.

Thompson was terribly badly burned and was too ill to be flown home, but with regular injections of a new drug called penicillin he made surprisingly good progress and seemed to be out of danger. His burns, however, were too extensive for real recovery, and although he was as gallant a patient as he had been an airman, cheerful and uncomplaining, enquiring every day after the rest of his crew and always managing to raise a smile, he died three weeks later from pneumonia in spite of the most dedicated efforts to save him.

For his splendid endurance and courage in getting the aircraft back safely, Harry Denton was awarded the DFC. George Thompson was posthumously awarded the Victoria Cross.

Only a man of great strength and will-power could have lifted a grown man from a jammed and blazing turret, standing almost directly over a gaping hole as he did so. Only a man of unique courage would have attempted it. His subsequent action in going to the aid of the tail gunner although burned beyond recognition himself saved the tail gunner's life at the ultimate expense of his own.

His action won him perhaps the most glowing panegyric in the long and eloquent history of VC awards. 'His courage,' said the citation, 'has seldom been equalled and never surpassed.'

# 3

## *The Maastricht Bridges*

FOR FORTY-EIGHT hours wave after wave of bombers, French and British, had pounded away at the two captured bridges over the Albert Canal in Belgium, two miles west of the Dutch border town of Maastricht. The canal banks were cratered but the bridges remained. Now, on the morning of 12 May 1940, forward elements of two panzer divisions were pouring across the two bridges in what looked like the main German thrust, threatening the whole Allied position on the north-eastern front. General Georges, the Allied Commander on this front, turned in desperation to Air Marshal 'Ugly' Barratt, C.-in-C. British Air Forces France, and pleaded with him to find some means of destroying the bridges.

All previous attacks had been made at night or from high level. There was only one way to make certain – a low-level attack in daylight. Barratt passed the task on to the Battles of No. 12 Squadron, based at the undulating grass airfield at Amifontaine, near Rheims in northern France. But in doing so he took an unprecedented step. It was a suicide job. No one was to go unless he volunteered.

The crews of 12 Squadron – the 'Shiny Twelfth', as they had been known in peacetime, but now more often the 'Dirty Dozen' – had had but a short experience of the *blitzkrieg*. Only two days earlier, pursuing the even tenor of their lives in the 'phoney' war, the officers had left the château in which they were quartered and gone into the village of Ami, where the NCO crews were billeted, for a party at the local *estaminet*, returning late at night to the château to sleep it off. Early next morning, 10 May, they had been awakened

56

by the sound of low-flying aircraft and gunfire. Pulling on odd garments of clothing over their pyjamas and dashing out into the courtyard, they had looked up at a dawn sky thick with Dorniers and Stukas and anti-aircraft fire. The 'phoney' war was over.

Momentarily stunned, they had taken cover in the woods surrounding the château. But sanity and nerve had soon returned and they had gone back to the château for a hurried breakfast before driving out to the airfield in the squadron bus. To their great surprise and relief they found the airfield unharmed. A big French base on the other side of the main road had been heavily bombed, but the grass of Amifontaine, whose buildings consisted of no more than a Nissen hut for an operations room and a circle of tents hidden in the forest, had not appealed to the Germans as any sort of target. Nor did it in the ensuing few days.

At 7.30 that morning orders were received from HQ. 'Belgium and Holland have been violated,' ran the message. 'Belgium has requested assistance from the Allies. Permission has been given for fighters to fly over the Low Countries, also reconnaissance aircraft. But not bombers. Bombers are to stand by.'

For the Battle squadrons of the Advanced Air Striking Force there followed an agonising wait. While the German columns poured through Holland and Luxembourg, and the *Luftwaffe* bombed and strafed targets in France, all Allied bombers were grounded, in a last blind, illogical hope, in the face of all the evidence, that the kid-glove war might continue. At midday Barratt's patience cracked and he ordered the bombing of enemy columns racing through Luxembourg. The Battles went into action and 12 Squadron were in the thick of it. By the end of that first day, of thirty-two Battles which took off to make bombing attacks, fourteen were lost and all the others damaged by gunfire.

Next day two main German thrusts were apparent. The first was aimed through Luxembourg and the Ardennes, the second through Maastricht, ninety miles to the north, towards Brussels. The French were confident that no armoured force could penetrate the dense forest of the Ardennes, a position of great natural strength, but to the north the Germans threatened to outflank the invincible Maginot Line and race across Belgium to the Channel ports.

A defensive line was quickly thrown along the Franco-Belgian frontier from the Maginot Line to the sea, and then this improvised line was swung northwards on its axis to meet the German advance, like the hour hand of a watch moving from ten o'clock to twelve. All the permanent bridges over the River Maas – or Meuse, as it was called in France – had been blown up by retreating Dutch and Belgian forces; but after German glider-borne troops had captured the two bridges over the Albert Canal west of Maastricht intact, the crossing of the Maas was effected by means of pontoon bridges. Troops, armour and supplies were now pouring across the canal, building up a powerful force inside Belgium and threatening to split the hurriedly positioned British and French forces and cut their way through to the sea.

Early on the morning of 12 May, the crews of 12 Squadron were called to the operations hut in the woods at Amifontaine. There they were met by the deputy squadron commander, Squadron Leader Lowe. There were representatives of some twelve crews in all, about thirty men packed into the long, narrow hut on the gently sloping hill above the airfield.

'The squadron has been specially chosen,' Lowe told them, 'to destroy a particularly vital target.' He explained the ground position and the vital importance of the two canal crossings. 'Six crews are to take off immediately to bomb these two bridges, three against each bridge.

'The Germans know the value of these bridges and they've had time to get their flak defences into position. You can expect the most obstinate defence, both from the ground and from fighters. But,' and he repeated the words of the operation order he had just received from headquarters, 'these two bridges must be destroyed at all costs.'

There was a ripple of animation, and then Lowe came to the point made by Barratt that no one was to go unless he volunteered. He had considered this carefully before deciding how best to present it. He had little doubt what the response would be, but losses had already caused some dismay, and this was clearly a death-or-glory raid. At this stage of the war morale was taken for granted, but Lowe had to guard against the very remote possibility that sufficient volunteers might not be forthcoming. He therefore phrased the question so as to leave the assembled crews little choice. 'The raid,' he said, 'will be carried out on a volunteer basis. Will anyone who doesn't wish to go please step forward.'

As he had expected, there was complete silence, with no movement of any kind. Then a volley of shouted appeals came from all parts of the hut, developing into a hubbub of pleading and cajoling as one by one the crews pressed their individual claims for going on the raid. 'Better put the names in a hat,' said someone, and the cry was taken up on all sides. But the most vociferous and insistent claims came from the six stand-by crews. 'It's our turn,' they objected, 'and we're ready to go. There's no call for volunteers.'

The acting squadron commander saw the force of this. So there was no lottery, no scribbling of names on slips of paper and lucky dipping into a hat. The six crews on the stand-by list won their point, and they went.

'Each flight of three aircraft will proceed independently to the target,' said Lowe, 'and each will have its own fighter cover. You will rendezvous with the fighters five miles southeast of Amifontaine.

'It's up to the two flight leaders, Thomas and Garland, to decide the most promising method of approach in each case, low-level or high dive. But remember – it's absolutely vital that we knock out these two bridges. At all costs. That's all.'

On the way out to their aircraft, the two flight leaders discussed their intended methods of attack. Flying Officer Donald Garland, a twenty-two-year-old Irishman from

County Wicklow, was leading his formation against the northernmost of the two bridges, a metal structure 370 feet long and 30 feet wide at Veldwezelt, on the road to Hasselt. Flying Officer Norman Thomas, a Dorset man, senior to Garland by about a year, was to lead his formation against a concrete bridge of the same dimensions a mile or so to the south at Vroenhoven, on the Maastricht–Tongres road. The concrete bridge presented the toughest resistance to the Battles' 250-pound bombs, but the metal bridge to the north required the deepest penetration.

'I'm going in at low-level,' announced Garland, as they shuffled across the grass airfield in their black leather flying-boots to the Fairey Battle aircraft, dispersed in the woods on the edge of the field. Tall, fair-haired and unassuming, tough but companionable, Garland was in many ways typical of the young short-service officer of his time. Only a slightly ironical, mocking sense of humour and a streak of unortho-doxy marked him out from his fellows. Although born in Ireland he had been educated in London and had been domiciled in Yorkshire until joining the RAF in 1937.

'You'll get shot to pieces at low level before you even reach the target,' said Thomas. 'Surely dive-bombing is the answer.' Thomas had joined the RAF in 1936 and had arrived in France on 2 September 1939 – one of the first RAF men to do so. Comparatively speaking he was an old hand.

'Low-level is the best way to achieve surprise,' said Garland.

'It hasn't had much success so far.'

'I still think it's better than going over at high level. It's the best way to avoid the flak and the fighters.'

Thomas made an attempt to rationalise his argument. 'On a clear day I might agree with you,' he said, 'but there's plenty of cloud about today. If we approach the target at high level and make use of cloud cover we'll have a better chance of getting through. Then if we make a last-minute dive at the bridges we shan't be so easy to shoot down over the target.'

'Dive-bombing is not so accurate,' said Garland.

'It *can* be just as accurate,' countered Thomas, 'and it gives you the speed you want for a quick getaway.'

The argument became heated as the clash of views continued. When they reached dispersal Thomas made a final effort to carry the day. 'We shan't be much use to anybody if we get shot down before we reach the target,' he said. But Garland refused to be persuaded, and in the end the two men agreed to differ. 'It'll be interesting to see the results,' said Thomas cheerfully as they separated to go to their aircraft. 'Let's hope we're both lucky enough to get back.'

The six pilots were Flying Officer Thomas, Pilot Officer Brereton and Pilot Officer Davy, of A Flight, and Flying Officer Garland, Flying Officer McIntosh and Sergeant Marland, of B Flight. Marland was one of the few men to enlist as a cook and butcher and graduate to a pilot's course. Joining the RAF in 1931, he had spent the next seven years overseas and had survived the Quetta earthquake of 1935. Wakened by the first rumblings, he had run clear of buildings in which many of his contemporaries had died. McIntosh was a wiry Australian, lean and muscular, with black hair and sallow complexion and a dark straggling moustache. Formerly a sheep farmer, he was of an even, cheerful temperament, and was the man who had hewn down most of the trees to make the aircraft dispersals on the edge of the forest. He was a fine woodsman and could fell a tree while other men stood thinking about it. Davy, tall, dark and slightly built, was only just out of school.

Each aircraft carried a crew of three, pilot, observer and gunner. The most experienced of the navigators was Sergeant Tom Gray, 'Dolly' Gray – tall and strongly built, blue-eyed and happy-go-lucky but deeply sincere underneath – who flew with Garland. Now 27, he had joined as an apprentice at 15 with a passion to fly. Another ex-apprentice navigator was Sergeant Neville Harper, who flew with McIntosh. All the gunners were ground tradesmen who had volunteered for flying duties just for the hell of it. Their duties included daily inspection of all aircraft radio and electrical installations, major and minor inspection schedules, the calibration of receivers and transmitters, battery charging, flare-path duty, ground-to-air wireless communications, telephone operating (they were the best informed men on any squadron) and training in gun-handling. They endured all this gladly and regarded themselves as privileged people because of the chance to fly. It certainly couldn't have been the money. When fully trained they got about £2 a week, and their bonus rate for flying amounted to 1s. 6d. a day.

And what of their aircraft, the Fairey Battle? All the pilots were agreed that it was structurally sound and of great strength, that it handled beautifully and was a superb aircraft to fly. But its single engine, its long greenhouse-type crew compartment, its slow speed, and its lack of modern defensive armament, marked it down as belonging to an earlier decade. Originally designed for a crew of two, pilot and observer, it had been modified to accommodate a gunner towards the rear, the observer moving to the bomb-well, where going into action he was stretched out uncomfortably on his stomach to operate his bomb-sight and his field of vision was limited. The armament consisted of one free gun fired by the gunner and a fixed gun firing rearwards from the well. To fire it the observer had to lean through the bombing aperture and take aim periscopically through a mirror.

Even as a night bomber the Battle was obsolescent. As a day bomber it was a sitting duck. This was the machine in which our highly trained peacetime pilots and crews were called upon to go into action against a heavily defended target whose destruction might turn the tide of the biggest land battle since 1918.

Thomas and Davy took off first, just before eight-twenty, and circled the airfield for a few minutes waiting for Brereton, the third man in the section, who found his radio unserviceable and transferred to another aircraft, only to be held up a second time by hydraulic failure. He was left behind. When Thomas reached the rendezvous with the fighters south-east of Amifontaine there were no fighters to be seen. Deprived of his No. 2 and bereft of fighter support, he nevertheless set course for the target. The phrase used in the operation order and repeated at briefing filled his mind. *The bridges must be destroyed at all costs.*

It was a bright, fresh May morning with thick but broken cloud at 5000 feet ranging across the sky. Thomas and Davy climbed steadily through the cloud and levelled out at 7000 feet, cruising at 160 miles an hour. In the clear air above the cloud the sun glinted on the aircraft canopies and picked out the contrasting shadow-shaded green and brown camouflage of the upper surfaces and the black paint underneath. Periodically the crews had a clear view of the ground through breaks in the cloud, making navigation quite straightforward. Sometimes to the west the cloud broke up altogether and they could see for miles.

Thomas was aiming to cross the Meuse south of Tongres and keep about twelve miles to the west of Maastricht as far north as Tronde before swinging east on the final approach. This meant that they would be over friendly territory right up to the actual attack.

Five minutes after Thomas and Davy took off, Garland, McIntosh and Marland followed. There was still no sign of the fighter support. In fact the fighters, having missed the rendezvous, were making their way to the target area with the object of drawing off any fighter opposition that might appear. Garland levelled off at 2000 feet, ready to drop down to ground level approaching the target. The two Battle formations did not establish contact and saw nothing of each other after take-off. Thomas was above the cloud and Garland below.

Everything went according to plan for Thomas and Davy for about half an hour. Then, a few miles south of Tongres, came the first shock. Flak began to burst a short distance

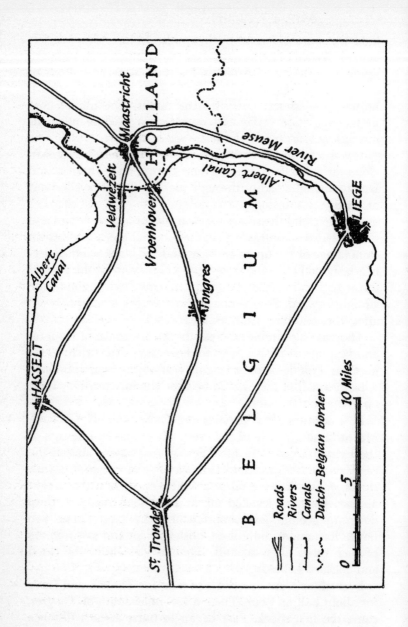

ahead of them, scattered at first, then more persistent. They had been told at briefing that the Germans had not yet crossed the Maas in strength, yet beneath them were German ack-ack units fifteen miles west of the river.

The detour via Tronde was now pointless. After a short conference with his observer, Sergeant Carey, Thomas altered course, steering north-east direct for the target. The flak began to thicken and he dropped down to 5000 feet, flying in and out of cloud to avoid enemy fighters, and taking evasive action to put the ground gunners off their aim. Davy tucked in close behind him. The effect of the flak bursts on the clouds was strangely horrific. They flew on through a cotton-wool inferno.

Suddenly about a mile to starboard they saw a formation of Blenheims being heavily attacked by flak. They were taking no evasive action so Thomas decided that they must be on their bombing run. Evidently British elements were already in contact with the forward German columns. The two bridges over the canal seemed more vital than ever.

As he came below the cloud Thomas got a glimpse of the town of Maastricht directly ahead, cut in half by the winding river. All the bridges over the river were down. The flak intensified. Then he saw the canal, picked out the Maastricht–Tongres road, running diagonally across his track, and followed it with his eye from left to right until it reached the canal. There was the concrete bridge he had been briefed to attack, trim and neat and unmarked.

He turned to starboard, skirting the western edge of the town, aiming to make his dive from the far side of the Canal and make a getaway to the south-west towards Belgium. But as he was about to dive into the attack his gunner, Sergeant Campion, called him on the inter-com.

'Enemy fighter closing in on the starboard side.'

The drill of the German ground gunners was impeccable. As the fighter closed in, all flak ceased.

Thomas signalled to Davy to warn him of the fighter, which was coming in slightly above them on the starboard beam. It looked as though Davy's aircraft would be the first to be attacked. The gunners, Campion in Thomas's aircraft, and LAC Patterson, a Canadian, in Davy's, each trained their single Vickers machine-guns on the fighter and waited for it to come within range, while the two observers strained their necks peering into their mirror-sights without seeing anything.

'He's having a go at Davy,' called Campion suddenly. 'He's chased him into cloud.'

Thomas now had a difficult split-second decision to make. Should he try to stay with Davy and offer what combined fire-power he could in defence against the fighter, or should he dive to the attack, hoping that Davy would be able to beat the fighter off and follow him down?

Again that phrase at briefing echoed in his mind. The bridge. He had to get the bridge. Everything, his own life, the lives of his crew, Davy's if it came to it, were subordinate to it. He pushed the nose of the Battle forward and dived on the canal.

His gaze settled hypnotically on the bridge and on a building on the far side. He aligned his aircraft so that the first part of the dive was fairly shallow, steepening the angle so that when he released the bombs the aircraft would be vertical. At 4000 feet he pointed the spinner of the propeller at the bridge and held on.

With one eye he watched the altimeter unwinding, while the Battle screamed and shuddered as it gathered speed. Carey, the observer, and Campion, the gunner, struggled to hold their position in the fuselage as the aircraft virtually stood on its nose.

In the bomb-racks were four 250-pound bombs, fused to explode instantaneously. Thomas released them individually in the dive, the first from 3000 feet and the last from less than 400 feet – dangerously low, so that he nearly blew himself up with the last explosion. Then he heaved back on the stick as hard as he dared.

The whole structure of the airframe strained and groaned

with the weight of the struggle as Thomas fought to pull out. Now the flak, which had been silent all the way down, opened up in unison from all directions, as though commanded by a single voice. As he pulled out and began a steep climb to 6000 feet for cloud cover he felt the aircraft stagger from the violence of the flak. It was as though some giant hand had closed around the fuselage and was shaking the aircraft to pieces. The wings would snap and the plane would disintegrate long before they reached the cloud.

He pushed the nose down again, completing the hump of a switchback, and threw the aircraft at the ground, flattening out giddily at twenty feet for a fast low-level getaway. Carey and Campion rolled and groaned with the strain of it. But the flak remained persistent and deadly accurate. They were hit again and again.

'Petrol's pouring into the aircraft!' called Carey. A shell had burst inside the starboard wing-root and splayed out all the fuel pipes leading into the fuselage. Carey grabbed the gushing petrol pipe and tried with his gloved fingers to staunch the flow.

Thomas held the throttle wide open, but the damaged engine, still for the moment getting a sufficient feed of petrol, carried them forward at its own speed. He watched the needle flickering around 90. Ground batteries and a road convoy were hammering away at them but he was too low to take evasive action. He knew how deep the German penetration was on this side of the Maas and he saw little hope of getting clear.

Suddenly the engine petered out altogether and the aircraft sank. A moment later, with the undercarriage still retracted, they touched down fairly smoothly in a field. The aircraft nosed forward. As soon as it came to a standstill Thomas jumped from the cockpit and ran back along the wing to check up on his crew. Although contorted and shaken they had both somehow escaped injury. Then he ducked as a hail of machine-gun fire beat against the fuselage.

67

'Stay where you are!' he yelled to Carey and Campion. He threw himself down in the grass beside the plane, looking round desperately for a ditch or some sort of shelter, but there was none. Even the grass was no more than two inches high and gave no protection. The hail of fire intensified and he watched Campion standing coolly by his gun, ignoring the fire, awaiting the order to open up. A hundred and fifty yards distant was the large enemy convoy they had seen from the air. The gunners seemed not in the least anxious to take them alive.

Amazed at Campion's courage, Thomas realised nevertheless that their position was hopeless and that to delay surrender meant certain death. As if to point the lesson a bullet ricocheted off the aircraft and struck him a glancing blow in the face. He got to his feet, raising his hands above his head as he did so. The firing ceased and a few moments later the German gunners strode across and took them prisoner.

Although Thomas had aimed his bombs at the bridge individually and with great deliberation, it was impossible in a high-dive attack to watch the bomb-bursts and he had no idea what damage he had done. He wondered how Davy had fared.

Patterson, Davy's gunner, had in fact shot down the fighter, and Davy had followed Thomas down in the dive. He was far enough behind to see the smoke and dust of Thomas's bombs settle and note extensive damage to the far end of the bridge.

Davy dived to 2000 feet before dropping his bombs, pursued by more fighters. As he turned for home he was attacked again by an Me 109, but Patterson's return fire was again accurate and eventually the German, emitting black smoke, disappeared through a gap in the clouds. Davy's aircraft, too, was badly damaged. Smoke was pouring from the port wing. 'It's the port petrol tank,' called Mansell, the observer. 'It's on fire.'

Looking over his shoulder at the burning wing, Davy

realised that the petrol tank might blow up at any moment. 'Prepare to abandon aircraft,' he called. Another look at the thick smoke streaming back from the wing decided him. 'Observer and gunner – jump!'

Patterson was the first to go. He struck the tail fin as he went and broke his ankle and wrist, but landed safely. Mansell followed and made a safe exit. The space of half a minute between their exit times meant the difference between five years in a POW camp for Patterson and escape behind the Allied lines for Mansell. But before he got back to base Mansell had an uncomfortable five minutes explaining to the hostile crowd which greeted his precipitate arrival at Liège that he wasn't a German.

As soon as Mansell and Patterson had gone, Davy began to think about his own exit. Then he noticed that the smoke from the wing was thinning out. The fire seemed to have stopped. He carried on towards base, eventually running out of petrol and landing in a field only a few miles short of Amifontaine.

During that day the captured Thomas and his crew three times crossed and re-crossed the bridge they had planned to destroy, as the Germans tried unsuccessfully to evacuate them east of the Maas. They saw craters on both sides of the bridge, one of which had reduced traffic to a single line, but the whole area was so extensively cratered that it was impossible to be certain that their attack had done the damage. The Germans showed great interest in the attack, trying to establish who had done it, but Thomas and his crew were careful to register surprise, managing to convince their captors that they had been on a reconnaissance flight.

*　　　*　　　*

Meanwhile Garland, McIntosh and Marland had flown northwards at 2000 feet for the first half-hour and dropped down to 50 feet nearing their target. Stretched out in the bomb-well, the three observers – Gray, Harper and Footner – saw nothing but a smooth river of green flooding past beneath them through the bombing aperture. Then suddenly they felt the aircraft shake and bump in what they at first took to be excessive turbulence. Soon they realised it was near-misses from the flak of German ground batteries that had already crossed the river.

There was scattered cloud at 1000 feet and Garland felt confirmed in his view that a low-level attack gave the best chance of success. He called McIntosh and Marland on the R/T. 'Fuse the bombs for eleven seconds delay,' he ordered. 'We're going in low level as planned.'

'Dolly' Gray judged the approach perfectly and soon they saw the neat Dutch town of Maastricht ahead of them, red-roofed and sturdy, its main square cut neatly out of the far bank of the river. In the distance, to the left of the town, lay the metal bridge across the canal which was their target, a mile or two north of the concrete bridge already attacked by Thomas and Davy.

'Form into line astern,' called Garland on the R/T.

Streamers of fire cut through the formation and tore sky-wards as the three Battles strung out into a long arrow and ploughed through a storm of flak and machine-gun fire. All three aircraft were hit repeatedly, but the thick light alloy deflector plate fitted along the bottom of the fuselage and the armour-plate fitted behind the pilots' and gunners' seats saved the crews from injury. Incredibly, the formation kept on.

Harper, McIntosh's observer, heard a shout on the inter-com and looking up from the bomb-bay saw a white ball of fire glowing beneath the pilot's seat where the fuel pipe passed across the fuselage. Suddenly it expanded into a wall of flame which blew back and enveloped him. Badly burned on the hands and face and suffering severely from shock, he thought only of getting away from the fire. Immediately behind him was the gunner's position, with a pivoting hood through which he made up his mind to crawl and jump clear. He had no parachute on, but he had to get away from the fire.

McNaughton, the gunner, guessed Harper's intention and stuck his body in the way, so that Harper couldn't get past. Meanwhile McIntosh had closed the pilot's hood, cutting down the draught, and the fire died down a little. Harper, recovering from the intensity of the shock and now well clear of the fire, calmed down and McNaughton eventually let him pass, allowing him to sit on the rear fuselage with his legs dangling into the cockpit, clinging on as best he could to McNaughton's parachute harness.

Choked with flames and smoke up front, McIntosh was forced to turn away from the target and jettison his bombs, attempting a belly-landing in a field to the left of the bridge. The landing was perfect and as soon as the aircraft stopped Harper slid over the side of the fuselage and landed on his back in the grass. Picking himself up quickly he rushed away from the aircraft. When he was clear of danger from the fire he looked down at his hands and saw that the skin was hanging from them like a pair of rubber gloves that had been pulled down and left dangling at the finger-tips.

Fighting hard against the nausea that attacked him, he suddenly realised that he was alone. The others must still be trapped in the blazing Battle. Turning round and starting back towards the aircraft, he saw McNaughton standing on the wing helping McIntosh to get out. McIntosh had burned his right hand in trying to operate the flap control lever, which had been enveloped in flames, and the burns were so bad that he was unable to release his straps. He owed his life to the gallant efforts of McNaughton, who rapidly untied the straps and pulled him to safety. A moment later both men were running across the grass to join Harper.

Looking again at the aircraft they saw that the whole fuselage was riddled with bullet-holes. The top of the engine cowling had been blown away completely and there were several holes the size of dinner-plates in the rear mainplane, while the fabric on the rudder and elevators was hanging in ribbons. The fire had taken a hold now and the ammunition had begun to explode.

The three men hid themselves in a trench running along the edge of the field, hoping to evade capture and make their escape at nightfall. McNaughton, who was unhurt, did what he could with the first-aid kits, but their condition was all against them. It was obvious that they wouldn't get far without help.

As they sat there bandaging each other's wounds they heard the sound of an aircraft to the north, and a moment later, over the tops of a line of trees to their right, there appeared a Battle, staggering along at fifty feet, flames pouring from the canopy and smoke trailing out to the rear. This they decided must be Marland, coming out of his attack on the bridge, hopelessly crippled but trying desperately to reach his own lines.

The three men in the ditch tensed and stood up as the Battle suddenly turned through ninety degrees and then pulled up almost vertically. For a moment it seemed to hang from the sky on its propeller. Then, falling on to its nose, it tore earthwards, crashed into the ground and blew up.

Marland's father had fought in the Boer War and had been exempt from military service in 1914–18, but had nevertheless joined up in 1916, only to be killed before the year was out – on the banks of the Albert Canal. His wife, left with three young children, had brought them all up with the aid of relatives to school-leaving age. The names of Marland's crew were Sergeant Footner and LAC Perrin.

A minute or so later the crew of the flak unit that had shot McIntosh and his crew down came along the edge of the trench and took them prisoner, escorting them to the local headquarters. 'You British are mad,' they were told when they got there. 'We capture the bridge early Friday morning. You give us all Friday and Saturday to get our flak guns up in circles all round the bridge, and then on Sunday, when all is ready, you come along with three aircraft and try to blow the thing up.'

'Did we succeed?'

The Germans wouldn't answer this one. But later that

day, when they were driven into Maastricht, they noticed that the ambulance made a detour and crossed the canal by another route.

Had Marland succeeded in hitting the bridge? And what had happened to Garland?

There is a story about Garland's attack which is impossible to substantiate. Yet it is fiercely believed by some of the men who were with him at Amifontaine.

The story relates how Garland's aircraft was badly hit by flak on the final run in. This is certainly confirmed by the experience of McIntosh and Marland. Garland himself was badly wounded, and so was Gray. Utterly determined to destroy the bridge, Garland fused his bombs to explode on impact, ordered his crew to bale out, and then dived his aircraft straight at the target and never pulled out.

The story, which is said to have been allowed to filter back to Allied Headquarters by the Germans themselves, is supposed to have come from Reynolds, Garland's gunner. Reynolds is said to have baled out successfully just before the attack, Gray being unable to do so because of his injuries. But this does not tie up with Garland's intention to approach and attack at low-level, which he certainly did; and Reynolds was killed in the attack, or he died immediately afterwards, for he was secretly buried by local Belgian patriots with the rest of the crew.

The only set of circumstances that would fit the story would be if Garland pulled up to give his crew a chance to bale out immediately before the attack but after McIntosh was shot down – and there was hardly time for this – and if Reynolds, although mortally injured through jumping from an insufficient height, survived long enough to pass the circumstantial details on to the Germans, who in their turn passed them on to the British. This sounds far-fetched, and no evidence can be found to support it.

The most likely interpretation is that Garland dropped his bombs as planned, from low-level and fused to explode eleven seconds later, but that in making certain of hitting the bridge he flew so low that he gave himself little or no chance of escaping. This, his comrades aver, is entirely consistent with the state of mind in which he approached the action.

It seems likely that Garland's aircraft crashed immediately beyond the bridge. One thing, however, is certain, Garland's formation severely damaged the bridge. To quote the RAF Short History, 'either Garland or Marland – and all the available scraps of evidence indicate that it was Garland – found the mark; for though the Battles lay broken and burning on the ground, the western truss of the bridge hung shattered in the air'. In a suicidal attack in impossible conditions, Garland's formation had achieved its allotted task.

For their leadership of the attack on this bridge, Garland and Gray were posthumously awarded the first air VCs of the war. In a poignant postscript to the operation, the RAF Short History remarks that since VCs were distributed sparingly, and there was no other appropriate honour which might be conferred on a dead man, Reynolds received no award. 'Let his name then at least stand recorded with those of his companions,' it says, 'in tribute not only to himself but to all the part-time air crew of the early days of the war.'

General Georges sent a personal signal to Barratt when he heard of the damage to the bridges. 'Je vous remercie,' he said simply. But what in fact did the attack achieve?

While it was claimed at the time that the damage to the bridges contributed in no small way to the subsequent miracle of Dunkirk, in retrospect it is clear that the Germans were already across the Maas in strength and that the temporary loss of one canal crossing and the damaging of another held them up but little. In any case, the main German attack developed not in this north-eastern sector but through the Ardennes, which the French had thought impregnable.

Recently a member of No. 12 Squadron who was shot

down two days after this attack revisited the little French village where his comrades were billeted and spent their leisure hours in the spring of 1940. He found the villagers touchingly interested in the fate of many young Englishmen long since dead and – elsewhere – hardly remembered.

Today at Amifontaine, a few rusting petrol cans are the only reminders of one of the great tragic operations of war, a gallant but pointless sacrifice which, like the Charge of the Light Brigade, will remain an inspiration to British arms long after many more brilliantly successful operations are forgotten.

# 4

## *Hughie Edwards*

THIRTIETH JUNE 1941 – and conditions for a low-level attack on the port of Bremen, for which two squadrons, Nos. 105 and 107, had been briefed, had become impossible. Wing Commander Hughie Edwards, the twenty-seven-year-old Australian commanding 105 Squadron, knew this well enough. A blanketing, blinding, smothering wall of fog shrouded the enemy coastline ahead and made the two Blenheims still managing to keep formation with Edwards look like wraiths. Fifteen Blenheims had started out on the raid but twelve had already lost formation and receded into the mist and fog. Yet Edwards still stayed on course. He was thinking of the events that had led up to the raid.

Two days before, under the leadership of another wing commander, Laurence Petley of 107 Squadron, the attack had got this far, and then Petley had turned back. That trip had begun and ended badly. First there had been a mechanical fault in Petley's aircraft. Rather than miss the rendezvous with 105 Squadron and compromise the whole operation, Petley had instructed his No. 2, a young pilot-officer named W. J. ('Bill') Edrich, to take over.

Over the North Sea at fifty feet the crews had spotted a Blenheim overtaking them. It was Petley. The relief of the young pilot officer was unbounded even at the time, but doubly so later, in the light of what followed.

It had been a perfect June day, with a cloudless sky, and approaching the enemy coast Petley had judged the operation as too hazardous altogether in the complete absence of cloud cover. This was in accordance with his briefing, anyway as he had understood it. The Blenheim was no match

76

for German fighters, and it was never ordered to penetrate into enemy territory in daylight to any depth without some sort of cloud sanctuary near at hand. Edwards had felt that having got so far they might have gone on, but the responsibility wasn't his and anyway he couldn't be sure what he might have done. Petley was a seasoned campaigner with a magnificent record and he knew what he was doing. They could always try again tomorrow.

Bill Edrich has gone on record as saying that there wasn't a man in the air who didn't agree with Petley.[1] But there *was* such a man on the ground – the air officer commanding the group, Air Commodore D. F. Stevenson. No sooner had 107 Squadron landed and reported to the operations room than Stevenson phoned and asked to speak to Petley.

What the AOC said is not recorded, but it was clear to the others that Petley was on the carpet for failing to lead them on to their objective. The inference was too much for Petley. 'Well, sir,' he burst out eventually, 'if that's what you think we'll do the whole bloody show again now.'

But the AOC had other ideas. He chose the same two squadrons to repeat the raid, but he changed the leadership. And on this second occasion Petley, chastened but still feeling that he had made the right decision, was flying behind Edwards. Fortunately the two men were old friends.

Frustrated by the fog, Edwards accepted the hopelessness of the situation. The plan for a full-scale attack had foundered, and the three remaining Blenheims could do little damage except to themselves. He had his own conscience to face, more important to him even than an angry AOC, and he gave the signal to break and turn for home.

When they got back there was another post-mortem, and another move to change the leadership. Edwards was called in front of his station commander, Group Captain 'Bertha' Battle.

'Are you still keen to lead this raid?' asked Battle.

'Very. I've had to turn back twice now, and I want to

[1] In *Round the Wicket* (Muller).

see it through.'

The station commander supported Edwards, and after some discussion he was retained as leader. One or two of the other crews, including Edrich, were sent north for a daylight raid on Sylt, but otherwise the composition of the raid remained substantially the same.

Both Petley and Edwards had fully appreciated that this was no ordinary raid. The choice of Bremen as a daylight target made that clear. But they could not read the minds of the air chiefs, and they had little idea of the critical questions of politics, prestige and morale that were involved. In the previous twelve months over 43,000 civilians had been killed in air raids on Britain. Churchill had promised that the RAF would retaliate by day and by night. And six days earlier Hitler had attacked Russia, and Churchill had at once called on the RAF to create a maximum diversion in the west. The night bomber force was already operating against land targets. Now the Blenheims were called upon to do the same – in daylight.

Churchill paid a personal visit to the Blenheim stations and gave the crews the unpalatable facts. Germany must be forced to move her fighters westwards. 'I am relying on you,' he said. So in demanding a tempo of leadership that bordered on rashness, the AOC was doing no more than fulfil the immediate policy of the War Cabinet.

Edwards, over six feet tall and of athletic build, had won the DFC a few days previously for a mast-height attack on shipping off the Dutch coast in which he had severely damaged and probably sunk a 4000-ton merchant vessel. Starting his operational career only five months earlier as a flight lieutenant, he had risen rapidly to wing commander because of heavy losses and his own fortuitous survival. Six wing commanders in No. 2 Group had been lost in one week. But the Edwards story went back a good deal farther than this.

Born in Australia in 1914 of a Welsh immigrant family, he had been a cadet pilot with the Royal Australian Air Force before transferring to the RAF in 1936. Then in 1938,

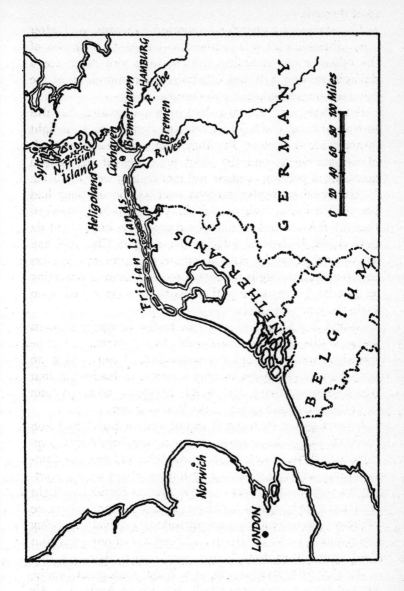

on a training flight, he had been caught out in severe icing conditions and his Blenheim had spun earthwards, out of control. In baling out he struck the tail-plane and his parachute fouled the rudder and tail-wheel. Spiralling downwards with the crashing Blenheim, he was only a few hundred feet up when he finally freed the rigging lines of his parachute and plummeted clear. A heavy landing meant further injuries and he spent the next two years in and out of hospital. The most serious injury was the severing of the main nerve of his right leg, causing paralysis from the knee down. He was told he would never fly again.

By persistence and persuasion he eventually managed to get some dual on both single and twin-engined aircraft, finally being pronounced fit to go solo on both types : and armed with this he badgered the medical board until they gave him a limited flying category. Then at last, in August 1940, he attained his goal – a full flying category, home and overseas.

But during night-flying training at Bicester – where by a strange coincidence his flight commander was Laurence Petley – he was caught out again, this time during an air raid, when all beacons and lights were switched off and radio contact ceased. Running out of petrol, he was left with the choice of baling out or flying his Blenheim down into the darkness. He chose to aim his aircraft into open country and bale out, but then found that the escape hatch was jammed. He had no alternative but to sit tight until he hit the ground. The darkness remained impenetrable, and with the altimeter reading zero he could still see nothing, but he had a miraculous escape, hitting a tree and suffering nothing worse than concussion. This held him up until early in 1941.

Now, after thirty-five operational trips, he was leading two squadrons on one of the most daring raids of the war. Even approaching Bremen from the north, as they planned to do, they would have to fly over enemy territory for 150 miles – an unprecedented daylight penetration in mid-1941.

The fifteen Blenheims took off at dawn on 4 July. Wellingtons and Whitleys had bombed Bremen during the hours of darkness and it was hoped that there would be a numbing of resistance after the night ordeal.

The two squadrons rendezvoused off the Norfolk coast. There were nine aircraft from 105 Squadron and six from 107, and Edwards led them across the North Sea in loose vics of three, flattened low on the water. He was aiming to keep well clear of the shipping lanes off the Frisian Islands and the North German coast and pass south of Heligoland before turning in to make a landfall west of Cuxhaven; then to skirt east of Bremerhaven before making a dash straight for Bremen. This way there was some hope of achieving surprise. But the weather was just the same as on the day when Petley had led them. There wasn't a cloud in the sky. German shipping approaching the estuaries of the Weser and the Elbe was almost bound to see them.

Soon the force of Blenheims began to thin out a little. Edwards was setting a fast pace of 200 knots, as briefed, and three of the 107 Squadron aircraft couldn't keep up. Left behind on their own, out of contact with each other, they turned for home. Now there were twelve.

North of Cuxhaven Edwards turned south and the formation began to run down towards the mouth of the Weser. Soon they saw their first ship. Edwards turned to port, away from the bows of the ship, hoping to avoid being seen, but another ship loomed up dead ahead, and then another still further to port. Ship after ship would now be reporting on them and all chance of surprise was gone.

Edwards picked his way between the ships as best he could to protect the formation from low-angle flak and cross fire, and they made their landfall as planned. Soon a railway track provided a check on their compass course.

The flight became deceptively peaceful as they crossed thousands of acres of flat farming country, while German farmers, mistaking them perhaps for a flight of Ju 88s returning from a raid, waved to them nonchalantly. It was the calm before the storm. A few minutes after skirting

Bremerhaven the crews could see the bowl of smoke-haze dead ahead that betrayed the proximity of Germany's second largest port. Then, suspended amongst the haze like lanterns, 2000 feet above the low-flying Blenheims, the crews saw innumerable sausage-shaped objects hanging lethally in the sky. The balloon barrage over Bremen was waiting for them, passively menacing.

Dangling from each balloon would be the deadly cables specially designed as a hazard to low-flying aircraft. The balloon sites were mobile, the exact positions of the balloons were dependent in any case on the wind, and it was impossible to plot a course to avoid them. They would simply have to plough through them, like a motor-car through a swollen ford, hoping to come out on the far side.

Affixed to each wing the Blenheims had a metal protrusion, like a pair of tree-pruners but with the scissors at the leading edge of the wing, which were supposed to energise when struck by a balloon cable, clutching the cable and cutting it through. But the effectiveness of this mechanism was doubtful, and in the minds of the crews the balloon cables were a hazard that had to be accepted.

They were approaching the docks at right angles. Edwards ordered the formation to spread laterally so as not to present a grouped target, and the twelve Blenheims charged towards the main dock area like some irresistible forward line, 1000-pound bombs at the ready all along the line. Ahead of them, in addition to the balloon cables, loomed all kinds of obstructions – pylons, high-tension cables, telegraph wires, gantries, warehouses, even the masts of ships. And now the flak had started, spasmodic at first, then faster and thicker than anything the crews had known, pouring at them in a continual stream. Light flak, machine-gun fire, heavy flak, poms-poms from the ships at the dock-side – all were directed at them indiscriminately. Suddenly a line of high-tension cables rushed at their windscreens. Some of the pilots pulled up over the top but Edwards hugged the grey slate roof-tops and ducked underneath. A huge pylon flashed by, missing his wing-tip by inches. None of the pilots deviated from their course for telephone wires and most aircraft collected yards of tangled cable. Early morning telephone conversations on the Bremen switchboard were rudely cut short.

Flying through a sleet of criss-cross flak and suffering repeated hits the twelve Blenheims raced on for the docks, spread so wide that each crew picked an individual target. Ahead they could see seamen and stevedores frantically taking cover behind buildings and sheds. Some, caught in the open, dived beneath stationary motor-cars. Then, in a crazy and haphazard jumble that yet seemed to have some pattern and order, the crews began disgorging their bombs, straddling the whole target area.

Factories and buildings and sheds shook and crumbled under the impact of high explosive, smoke and steam poured from the wharves, twisted metal from the gantries and railheads clawed in lifelike agony towards the sky. The whole dock area was an inferno of fire and smoke and debris and hissing steam. But already the attacking force was paying the price. One aircraft, belching smoke and fire, crashed into a warehouse and blew up, flinging debris up through the formation and skywards to a height of 500 feet. The NCO crew had completed their training and joined the squadron only a fortnight earlier : the Bremen raid was their first trip. Another aircraft from 105 Squadron, streaked with flame, turned inland to escape the flak and was not seen again.

Not a single aircraft escaped severe damage. The heaviest losses were on the port side of the formation, where Petley and the other two 107 Squadron crews formed the left wing. Of these three crews only one survived. The gallant Petley, who had never forfeited the absolute confidence of his crews and comrades, was seen to crash in flames.

But the remaining crews weren't finished yet. Several still had bombs on board and were searching for likely targets. They waited until they flew near factories and railway junctions and planted their bombs as they went. One bomb burst in a timber yard and threw a pile of planks into the air like a box of matches. The following aircraft cut through a barrage of falling timber. A goods train that stopped and opened up at Edwards got a burst from the leader's front gun as he swerved towards it, scattering the gun-crew. Another pilot found an airfield on the way out and machine-gunned a line of Ju 88s.

Bremen, taken by surprise after all, had been about to lick its wounds after the night's raid. Now, like a boxer struggling to his feet to beat the count, it had suffered another knock-down. Leaving the dockside devastated and the city cowed and confused, the eight surviving Blenheims withdrew.

Many of the crews were wounded, many of the aircraft were written off after landing, but two-thirds of the force had returned to base from an attack on one of the most heavily defended targets in Europe. In spite of a clear sky and the certainty that their approach was known, Edwards had plainly earned a high honour. A fortnight later he was awarded the VC. His navigator, Pilot Officer Ramsay, later lost at Malta, was awarded the DFC and the wireless operator/air gunner, Flight Sergeant Gerry Quinn, who collected a cannon-shell splinter in his knee, got a bar to a previously-awarded DFM.

British accounts of the raid hailed it somewhat prematurely as the beginning of a round-the-clock bombardment of German cities; but the impact of the raid on the Germans was so great that Goebbels was stung into issuing a special communiqué. 'The slight military damage that was caused,' he said, 'could be quickly repaired.' (He did not say that it *was*.) 'Five of the attacking aircraft' – Goebbels had included a Wellington lost the previous night – 'were shot down, three Blenheims crashing over Bremen itself.' Goebbels then added a telling comment. 'To lose five out of twelve attacking planes is equivalent to a serious reverse, which no amount of propaganda can turn into a success.'

It was true enough that no force could operate for long with such losses. But this had been more than just another raid. It had been a symbol of Britain's determination to repay the German air blitz in full one day, and of her readiness to accept heavy losses in an attempt to divert the *Luftwaffe* from the Russian front.

Three weeks after this raid Edwards took a squadron to Malta for a tour of operations against enemy shipping in the Mediterranean. The squadron was virtually wiped out while it was there. Edwards came back to do a tour on Mosquitoes, and later he did a third tour on Lancasters. He led the famous raid against the Philips factory at Eindhoven in December 1942, winning the DSO and drawing from King George VI the comment that he was the first man to win all three medals – VC, DSO, DFC – in World War II. Later he was joined in this distinction by Guy Gibson and Leonard Cheshire.

His view of decorations is best summed up in his own words. 'This is your VC,' he told the surviving crews after the Bremen raid. He was thinking, too, of the men who had not returned. 'I was simply the person to be presented with it.'

## *The Outback Aussie*

FLIGHT SERGEANT Ron Middleton, twenty-six-year-old Australian from Yarra Bandi, New South Wales, eased the stick of the old four-engined Stirling bomber back into his stomach for the twentieth time. It was no good. He couldn't squeeze another foot out of her. A Stirling ought to reach at least 16,000 feet, even with a full bomb load. Yet the ceiling of this aircraft, 'H for Harry', seemed to be no more than 12,000. It wasn't enough.

Between them and their target, the Fiat Works at Turin in Northern Italy, lay the towering switchback of the Alps. Right on track, at 15,782 feet, rose the pointed summit of Mont Blanc. Several other massive peaks jutted into the sky ahead of them, perilously near. And there was no moon to help them thread their way through the mountain passes. They needed another 5000 feet to be safe.

Even in the climb to 12,000 feet across France Middleton had been warned by Jeffery, his six-foot-four flight engineer, formerly a Halton apprentice and still only eighteen, that they were using up too much fuel. Once across the Alps they would have to come down to low level to stand any chance of hitting the Fiat Works. Then they would be faced with another struggle for height to negotiate the Alps on the homeward trip. If fuel consumption continued at the present rate they would never get back.

The raid was part of the Allied strategy of keeping the Italians at full stretch while the British and American forces landed and secured a foothold in North Africa. On this night, 28/29 November 1942, 183 Bomber Command aircraft had Turin as their target. Of these, seven specially selected crews of No. 149 Squadron had been briefed to bomb the Fiat Works at low level. Of these seven, three had already been forced to turn back through fuel and icing troubles.

Middleton called Mackie, his front gunner. 'Keep a look-out ahead.' The rest of the crew joined in the vigil, peering out through the darkness at the black slopes of the mountains. Below them, glimpses of jagged, rocky mountain-tops alternated with chasms of indigo. Patches of snow, luminous among the dark shadows, gleamed on the higher slopes. But mostly they stared into a wall of impenetrable darkness, tense with the threat of high ground.

Nothing more was said as the Stirling nosed its way forward between the peaks. This great natural barrier had been the graveyard of many a bomber crew. But Middleton was not turning back.

Dark-haired and good-looking, lean, tough and unassuming, Middleton had worked as a 'jackaroo' before the war at the Wee Wang Sheep Stations at Brogan Gate, New South Wales, where his father was manager. Joining the Royal Australian Air Force in 1940, he had been the earnest, plodding type of pupil, steady and thorough if unspectacular. Early in 1942 he had completed his training in Canada and joined 149 Squadron at Lakenheath as a second pilot. Introspective and reticent, subject to fits of melancholy, with a strong preference for his own company, he was in many ways the typical outback Aussie. Then, on the night of 6 April 1942, came an incident which changed him completely.

He was second pilot of a Stirling in a raid on Essen. Over the target they were caught in the searchlights and then attacked by a night fighter. Again and again the fighter bored in, tearing chunks out of the starboard wing and setting fire to an engine. The crippled Stirling limped back to base and broke up completely on landing. It was the sort of experience that unnerved the best crews. But Middleton reacted differently. The incident had an astonishing effect on him. It roused him out of his melancholy and galvanised him into a buoyant, companionable mood which never left him.

The metamorphosis was never explained. Perhaps Middleton's introspective melancholy had been inspired by self-doubt – lack of faith in himself and in his courage. That night over Essen he conquered his fear.

At the end of July he walked into the Sergeants' Mess at Lakenheath wearing a broad grin. He had been promoted to captain and allotted a crew. And after several trips as captain he was posted with his crew to the Pathfinder Force.

One morning after a trip to Nuremberg the flight commander sent for him. 'You've made the grade,' he was told, 'but one or two of your crew aren't quite up to it yet. I'm sending the whole crew back to 149. You'll be given a new crew here.'

'I won't be parted from my crew,' said Middleton doggedly.

The flight commander took in the set of the Australian's jaw. The chap was a fool but he couldn't help admiring him. He let him go back to 149.

Steadily Middleton and his crew worked their way through their operational tour. Rostock, Lübeck, Hamburg, Frankfurt, Munich, the Ruhr – all were visited, some many times. Then came a succession of long flogs over the Alps to targets in Northern Italy. The three gunners, Mackie in the front turret, Cameron in the mid-upper and Gough in the rear, got in several extra trips due to a shortage of gunners, and they completed their thirtieth trip early in November. But they did not forget Middleton's loyalty to the crew, and they volunteered to stay on until the whole crew was safely through. This trip to Turin was Middleton's twenty-ninth operational sortie. The last but one.

'Mountain straight ahead,' called Mackie from the front turret.

Middleton discerned a dark shape which filled his windscreen, darker even than the sky. There seemed to be no

88

way round it. He looked quickly left and right. Tall sentinel peaks blocked their path in all directions. They were trapped.

There was only one way to get extra lift quickly, and that was to jettison the bomb-load. It would mean an anti-climatic, abortive end to the whole perilous mission. But it was either that or crash the plane into the mountain. Middleton selected bomb-doors open and called Royde, the navigator. 'Get ready to jettison the bombs, George. Looks like we're coming to a dead end.'

Suddenly there was an excited shout from the front turret. 'It's there! Look! To starboard!' Through a narrow mountain pass far to the right they caught a glimpse of the twinkling lights of Turin, several miles distant and thousands of feet below, the flares of the Pathfinders already blazing in the sky above the city. Middleton closed his bomb-doors, swung the Stirling to starboard, and aimed for the pass.

For three more agonising minutes the Stirling scraped along less than a hundred feet clear of the stark summit rocks that separated them from the pass. Then the ground fell away beneath them and there was a moment's glorious relief before they settled down to begin their run up to the target.

'What's the fuel situation now?' asked Middleton.

'We shall have a head-wind on the way back,' answered Jeffery. 'If we come down for a low-level attack we may not get back to base.'

'Could we make an airfield in southern England?'

'We might.'

'All right. We'll go down.'

Middleton began to take the Stirling down into the turmoil over Turin. The hazards ahead, in addition to the flak, included the bombs of the main force, bombing from high level, and the pendant flares of the Pathfinders, suspended in the sky. Royde, the navigator, crawled into the bombing well, while Middleton weaved his way skilfully down towards the centre of Turin, somehow avoiding the tangle of

89

white silk parachutes and shroud-lines from which the flares were hanging.

As they crossed the perimeter of the city they began to encounter indiscriminate flak which seemed to leap at them with a kind of centrifugal force from the hub of the city. Then as they neared the target the flak intensified and became more personal. The ground gunners had picked out the low-flying plane and were intent on shooting it down. Suddenly the whole aircraft staggered with the shock of a direct hit in the port mainplane from a heavy-calibre shell.

Struggling to keep control, Middleton glanced out of his window and saw a huge gaping hole in the wing. It had reduced lift and thrown the aircraft off balance. 'Come and help me hold her straight!' he called to Hyder, his second pilot. The two men worked feverishly at the controls until they evolved a reasonable trim. But in the confusion they lost sight of the target.

'We're still OK,' Middleton reassured his crew. 'I'm going to have another go at finding the target.' And they began circling again amongst the flak.

It was a wonderful night for area bombing, dark but with no low cloud, and with the target brilliantly illuminated by the flares. But drifting smoke and flame from the high-explosive and incendiaries dropped by the main force made locating their pin-point target difficult. It was two or three minutes before they identified the Fiat Works, levelled out at 2000 feet, and started their bombing run.

They were less than a mile from the target. Middleton and Hyder sat together in the cockpit, holding the Stirling on a steady course. Royde was stretched out in the bomb-well, waiting for the target to appear in his bomb-sight. Meanwhile the three gunners fired repeatedly at the network of light flak posts that surrounded them. But with less than a quarter of a mile to go, the front windscreen burst asunder and a shell exploded in the cockpit, concussing the two pilots and shattering their precarious control.

There was a blinding light and then, for Middleton, complete darkness. 'I'm hit,' the others heard him say on the inter-com. Then he fell forward over the stick. He was badly wounded in the body and legs, and his right eye had gone, the flesh surrounding it torn away, exposing the bone. The Stirling lunged forward into a dive straight at the target, hurling everything forward inside the fuselage, while the slipstream, converted suddenly into an icy gale, tore through the smashed windscreen and screamed through the fuselage like a tornado.

Hyder, badly injured himself, fought to wrench Middleton clear of the stick and regain control. The rest of the crew, blasted by the slipstream and unaware of Hyder's struggles in the cockpit, braced themselves for the crash.

They were down to five hundred feet before Hyder was able to free the controls of Middleton's dead weight and level out. Caught in a hail of anti-aircraft fire, the Stirling was hit again and again. Gough, in the rear turret, and Skinner at the radio, were both wounded. Hyder ducked his head into the slipstream and tugged desperately at the controls, fighting for altitude.

As they climbed clear of the target Middleton, exerting his will against waves of unconsciousness, began to come to. His first words came haltingly, mechanically, from somewhere in the back of his throat. 'Are we too low to bomb?'

In spite of their appalling injuries, these two men now coaxed the crippled Stirling back towards the target at 1500 feet, while Royde, still waiting in the bomb-well, prepared once again to drop the bombs. Meanwhile thuds of light flak spattered along the fuselage continuously,

The Stirling, badly holed in one wing, half its rear turret shot away, with four men wounded and the whole crew buffeted as though in a wind-tunnel, lurched across the target for the third time. Not until the bombs were gone and they were climbing away from the target did Middleton and Hyder look at each other and size up their situation.

At once Middleton saw that Hyder, too, was badly wounded. 'Get back to the rest bunk to have your wounds dressed,' he ordered. 'I'll keep her going.'

Hyder, his left leg torn open, limped back through the fuselage and collapsed on the bunk. Jeffery and Skinner dried and cleaned his head-wounds with gauze, dresse his torn hands with a pad, and decided that his leg needed a tourniquet. But Hyder refused. 'There isn't time,' he said. 'I want to go back and help Ron.' And he got up from the bunk and shambled forward, head down, the blood-stains on his flying-suit showing up bright red as they caught the lights on the engineer's panel. Skinner, wounded in the leg himself, could not imagine how Hyder kept standing.

There were several courses now open to Middleton. He could turn south and make for North Africa, avoiding a second crossing of the Alps; but airfields had hardly been established there and in any case this meant a long sea crossing. He could force-land somewhere in Switzerland and face internment, with the possibility of subsequent escape back to Britain. Or, if the aircraft still responded fairly well and there was a chance of clearing the mountains, and if he could withstand the pain from his eye and the icy slipstream, he could start back towards England, risking the German night-fighter patrols over France, hoping to get down somewhere on the flat plains of France if anything went wrong. The last course was the most hazardous, but all his training pointed towards it. It was so tempting to take the easy way out, to turn back on the way out to the target, or make for a neutral haven when one's aircraft was damaged. But he knew that the continuance of bomber operations depended on the determination of pilots to bomb their targets and get their aircraft back to base.

He called Royde. 'Give me a course to steer to cross the Alps. Then jettison everything you can. We'll start climbing and see how high she'll go.'

Royde came up with the course and then went back into the fuselage to supervise the jettisoning of equipment. They threw out chunks of armour plating, oxygen bottles, ammunition, flares, spare seats, the camera, even the fire extinguishers and sextant. Royde went round with a fireman's axe, chopping off things to jettison. All they kept were their parachutes and their dinghies, in case at the last they were forced to bale out or come down in the sea.

When there seemed to be nothing movable left, Royde called Middleton. 'How are we doing?'

'She's climbing well.'

'What about the guns? Two in the tail turret have been shot away. Shall we jettison the rest?'

'Yes, George,' came the whisper, 'carry on. But try not to talk to me. I can't answer.'

They had a four-hour flight ahead of them, if their petrol held out, with all kinds of hazards facing them on the way and at the end. But with the aircraft lightened by the dropping of the bomb-load, the steady consumption of petrol and the ruthless jettisoning of equipment, they climbed to 14,000 feet and crossed the Alps safely, threading their way for the second time through the higher peaks. Middleton was almost blind now, Hyder was weak from the loss of blood, and both men were almost paralysed with cold, so Mackie, the front gunner, came back to help them steer the compass course and guide them through the mountains.

Then came the long flight across France, while the flight engineer kept a continual check on their petrol consumption and estimated their chances of reaching southern England. 'We ought to reach the French coast,' he announced at length, 'but I doubt if we'll get across the Channel.'

Once again there was the temptation to take the easy way, to bring the aircraft down safely in France, or bale out, without risking the Channel crossing in a crippled aircraft. But Middleton kept on. At no stage did any one of his crew question his decisions, even mentally. They had complete faith in him.

Obsessed with the need to conserve fuel, Middleton throttled back as they approached Paris and began a long let-down aimed at the English coast. This was the best way to make use of their height. But over northern France

93

Skinner, working the radio, saw a flash of light through the astrodome above him. Searchlights. They were down to below 7000 feet now, and twelve probing beams were holding them steady, like a series of tripods. Soon the flak found them, bursts of shrapnel rattled on the mainplane, and Middleton called on his last reserves of strength to throw the Stirling clear. All his plans for conserving petrol evaporated as the defenders boxed him in with accurate fire and forced him to swerve and jink and then dive away to the right to escape the blinding searchlight beams. He came out of the dive at last in merciful darkness, but at 600 feet.

And now to cross the Channel.

In spite of the severe damage suffered by the Stirling it was still flying strongly, and their only worry was fuel. To avoid the coastal guns they crossed the French coast south of Boulogne and then aimed for Kent. In fifteen minutes they would be there.

The night was still dark, but the moon had risen and occasional shafts of silver pierced the high cloud and glistened on the water. No one spoke as the minutes ticked by. They had been airborne for eight and a half hours. The time was a quarter to three.

A darker line on the water ahead of them told them that England was in sight. There was no light to guide them. As Middleton, Hyder and Mackie pointed the coastline out to each other the inter-com sprang to life. It was Jeffery.

'We've got another five minutes,' he said, 'I think I can guarantee that. But not ten.'

Five minutes. That would get them to the coast, but no farther. It meant baling out as soon as they got there. 'Give me my parachute,' called Middleton. His voice was thick and muted now, difficult to understand. Royde passed him his parachute, and they all clipped on their chutes. Skinner, at the radio, went off the inter-com to get a bearing. It might be important to know exactly where they were.

Middleton called the crew again, his voice attenuated to the merest whisper. 'As soon as we're over land . . . I shall turn parallel to the coast . . . and give the order to bale out. When everyone has gone . . . I shall turn the aircraft out to sea . . . and bale out myself. I don't want to risk the aircraft crashing into houses.'

As they crossed the coast Jeffery called Middleton. 'That's it, Ron. She'll die out any time now.'

'Prepare to bale out,' called Middleton. He took the Stirling a quarter of a mile inland and then turned east-north-east parallel with the coast. Half a minute later he called again. 'All right – jump, everybody.'

Skinner, switching back to the inter-com to give a bearing to Royde, found that he had missed the order. Meanwhile Mackie half-dragged, half-carried the badly wounded Hyder to the hatch and wrapped his fingers firmly round the parachute release handle before pushing him out. Skinner went forward just in time to see Hyder's upturned face disappear through the hatch. Gough, Cameron and Royde followed, and then it was Skinner's turn. In spite of his injuries he made a good exit.

As these five men fell away from the Stirling and their parachutes opened, they saw the aircraft bank gently and turn out to sea. What happened next must be conjecture.

Middleton must have realised that his injuries were serious and that he might not recover from them. He had probably survived this far on will-power alone – the determination to get his crew back safely, and the aircraft as well if he could. He was equally determined, now, not to risk the lives of civilians. He therefore gave everyone time to get clear and then turned the Stirling out to sea, knowing that his own chances of escape were infinitesimal. But he reckoned without the intense loyalty of his crew – the loyalty which his own actions and character had done so much to inspire. Mackie, who had stood behind him to help him fly the aircraft all the way from Turin, refused to leave him. So too, feeling that he might still be able to help him, did Jeffery, the eighteen-year-old flight engineer.

Perhaps in those last seconds of a dying aircraft there was

95

an argument amongst the skeleton crew – the first time one of Middleton's decisions had ever been queried. Middleton, a dying man himself, insisted with his last flicker of will-power that they go; and Mackie and Jeffery could not find it in themselves to disobey him further. They got ready to jump, but as they did so the engines finally sucked the petrol tanks dry.

When the engines of a big bomber cut, the aircraft did not always glide easily. Probably it lunged forward as Middleton tried to keep control, intent now on making a successful ditching. Meanwhile, driven by a last order from Middleton, Mackie and Jeffery jumped. But it was too late. Either the aircraft was too low for their parachutes to open properly, or they got out safely but died of exposure during the night. Their bodies, attached to open parachutes, were washed up next day.

As the five survivors twirled silently down to safety they watched the Stirling crash into the sea a mile off-shore.

It was two months before the wreck of the Stirling broke up and released the last member of the crew. Middleton's body was washed up off Shakespeare Cliff, Dover, on 1 February 1943. A fortnight earlier his unexampled devotion to duty had been recognised in the award of the Victoria Cross.

John
Nettleton

John Garwell

'Flap' Sherwood

'Darky' Hallows

Paul Cutting

Ron Irons

Eric Rodley

E. A. Deverill

1.

2.

4.

1. George Thompson

2. Harry Denton

3. Haydn Price

4. Ernie Potts

3.

The Dortmund-Ems Canal: above, on Christmas Day, 1944; below, after the raid on New Year's Day, 1945

Donald Garland

Tom Gray

Thomas's Battle after the crash

Fred Marland

Norman Thomas

A formation of Bristol Blenheims

Hughie Edwards

Low level attack on Bremen

Ron Middleton

Norman Skinner

The Short Stirling

L. A. Hyder

A. W. Gough

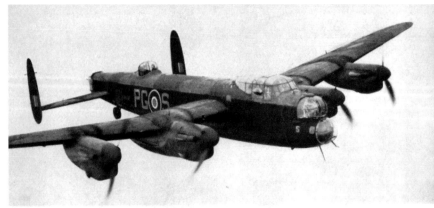

The Avro Lancaster

Norman Jackson

Jackson's Crew: Frank Higgins, Maurice Toft, Hugh Johnson, 'Sandy' Sandelands and Fred Mifflin

Mickey Martin

Hugh Maltby

Guy Gibson

The breached Mohne Dam and (inset) a reconnaissance photograph taken be

he raid

Arthur Aaron

Bill Reid and Les Rolton

Aaron's crew in tropical kit after the crash. Left to right: 'Mac' McCabe, Jim Richmond, Allan Larden, Malcolm Mitchem, Jimmie Guy

A flight of Mosquitoes at low level

Charles Pickard

Bill Broadley

The attack on Amiens Gaol

After the raid

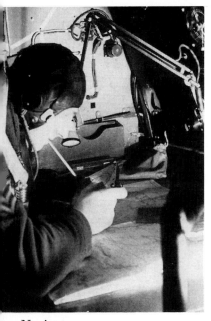

Navigator

Bomb aimer

Wireless operator

# 6

## *Guy Gibson*

THE MUTED roar of 200 Lancasters at 15,000 feet slowly
receded, leaving the little Dutch town of Steenbergen
alone to its midnight stillness and silence. Its 5000 citizens
slept. Only a few light sleepers tossed restlessly, aware that
the comforting drone that had been the background to their
dreams had evaporated. For to these Dutchmen the sound
was indeed a comfort, presaging as it did the final destruction of Nazi Germany and their own longed-for liberation.
Such a joyous outcome was worth many a sleepless night.

Two hours earlier they heard the Lancasters fly over, as
they so often did nowadays, on their way to targets in the
Ruhr. Somehow on the outward trip the sound of the
engines was different – pulsating, threatening, strident. On
the return flight the engines seemed to assume a warmer
tone, a throb of achievement, the satisfied hum of dangers
overcome and of duty done. There was sometimes, too, a
thinner echo, reflecting the loss rate to the sensitive ear.

Silence and sleep settled again on Steenbergen. Yet one
man at least remained awake.

Anton de Bruyn, night-watchman at the local sugar factory, had long surrendered his mind to a blanket of sound
that lay over the town. The term night-watchman was a
misnomer. In darkness, sight was a secondary perception
to the tympanum of the ear. Heat and light might travel
faster that sound, but there was no doubt at night which
was the closer friend. Anton de Bruyn was a listener.

He listened until the last decibel of sound from the Lancasters ebbed away. The leaders must now be well over the
North Sea, almost in sight of home. He was glad for them,

97

shared for a moment in their tired elation. Then the beginnings of another sound, distant and yet comparatively near, demanded his attention.

It was the sound of an aircraft, and yet it was no ordinary sound. The full-throated roar of the Lancaster had been succeeded by the nasal snarl of the fighter – or so it seemed. Perhaps it was a German night-fighter, chasing a stray Lancaster. But something about the sound suggested urgency. For a moment the aircraft engines were something more than inanimate. They gave out the call of a wounded animal, transmitting a cry for help to all who could hear. It was the sound of an aircraft in trouble.

The night-watchman hurried out of the factory and into the street. Here the sound was deafening. It would wake the whole town. The sound-waves seemed to strike him equally from all directions, as though he were the pivotal point, or some sort of target. Suddenly he saw what he took to be the shadow of an aircraft, low over the roof-tops to the east. Then he saw that what he had taken for the shadow was the substance. It was a low-flying twin-engined aircraft, which he rightly guessed was a Mosquito, and it was circling the town. The aircraft seemed to carry its own illumination, and in what he took to be the glow of the cockpit lights he could clearly see two silhouetted figures, hunched together, staring down, looking perhaps for a pinpoint, or searching for a place to land.

Anton de Bruyn could not know that the man flying the Mosquito had controlled that night's raid as master bomber, the same man who sixteen months earlier had pioneered this form of raid control in the legendary dam-busting raid, the man who by common consent was the greatest of all bomber pilots, Guy Gibson. It was 19 September 1944.

*　　　*　　　*

Guy Gibson was born in Simla, India, in 1918, the son of a government forestry official. He was educated in England, at St George's School, Felixstowe, and St Edward's School,

Oxford. He was not outstanding either as a student or games player, though his thoroughness and determination made him, in the opinion of the Warden at St Edward's, one of the most purposeful boys ever to attend the school.

Once Gibson had set his mind to a thing nothing could move him. In 1935, while still at school, he applied to join the RAF. Of below average height, he was rejected because of his short legs. Yet a year later he persuaded the RAF to accept him as a pupil pilot, and he was commissioned in the following year.

He was twenty-one when the war began, and at twenty-three he was commanding one of the leading squadrons in Bomber Command. By this time his personality was complete. A cheerful spirit that was infectious, a pink-cheeked, boyish grin, a firm handshake, the inevitable pipe, a direct manner, wasting no words, the ability to let his hair down and relax on a thrash with the boys and yet retain that streak of ruthlessness which demanded respect – all these combined to make him the very image and epitome of the young RAF war-time leader. And he was so obviously a warm human being. A lover of animals, he was recognisable always at a distance from the black Labrador 'Nigger' clinging to his heels, a dog he had had from a pup.

By March 1943 Gibson had completed his second tour of bombing operations, totalling seventy-eight flights over enemy territory. Between these two tours he had sandwiched a hundred defensive night-fighting sorties when technically he should have been enjoying an operational rest. He still had no wish to come off operations, but his commanders insisted. So inevitably he relaxed. The daily prospect of sudden death receded. His mind began to get accustomed to the idea of the continuance of life, at least for a period. He began to think about some leave – a long, carefree holiday with his wife, whom because of the rigours of his operational career he rarely saw. It was at this point that a conversation took place between Air Chief Marshal Sir Arthur Harris, Commander-in-Chief Bomber Command, and Air

99

Vice-Marshal the Hon. Ralph Cochrane, Gibson's group commander.

'I've got a job for you, Cocky,' said Harris.[1]

Harris went on to explain the details of a new bomb invented by a scientist named Barnes Wallis and the nature of the target suitable for the bomb's capabilities. He then announced his intention of forming an élite squadron of experienced men for a single raid on the Mohne and Eder dams, the Ruhr's main water suppliers and important sources of hydro-electric power.

'Have you got anyone in particular in mind to command such a squadron?' asked Cochrane.

Harris met Cochrane's question with the air of a man whose mind has long been made up. 'Yes. Gibson.'

It was left to Cochrane to send for Gibson. After congratulating him on the award of a bar to his DSO (he was already a double DFC), Cochrane came to the point.

'How would you like the idea of doing one more trip?'

Gibson had been off operations for no more than a week or so – nothing like long enough to develop the restless urge for squadron life which later attacked him. He had been posted to group headquarters – so he had been told – to write a book on his part in the bomber offensive. He was finding it difficult to settle down, but he was approaching the task with typical thoroughness. Now it seemed that he was to be thrust once more amongst the flak and the fighters. He was mentally quite unprepared for Cochrane's question.

'What kind of a trip, sir?' He was parrying the blow, giving himself time to think.

'A pretty important one, perhaps one of the most important of the war. I can't tell you any more now except that you would lead it.'

The operational side of Gibson, his real self, the self he had suppressed to do this desk job, was reasserting itself. But his thoughts were still confused and incoherent as Cochrane fired his final question.

[1] As recorded in Paul Brickhill's *The Dam Busters.*

'Well – do you want to do it?'

'I think so, sir. Yes.'

'Good. I'll let you know more about it as soon as I can.'

Gibson's certainty that he would not return from the dams' raid was in a sense protracted and cumulative and in a sense sudden and dramatic. It began with this need to screw his courage to the sticking place again after deliberately relaxing the tension. Later he learned the nature of the targets with relief. It seemed to him that it could have been so much worse. He began to hope that he might get back. Then he became absorbed in the training task, learning and planning and scheming and flying, far too busy for selfish thoughts of his own survival. Indeed the difficulties of making the raid a success were so stupendous that they completely engaged the thoughts of those involved, both on the ground and in the air, during the weeks of preparation, leaving no time for morbid fears. It was not until literally the eleventh hour, on the night before the raid, that it suddenly occurred to Gibson that he might not get back – that indeed none of them might get back, that in the process of attempting to destroy the two dams the whole squadron might be wiped out. And once the dangers of the operation were remembered at all, they immediately assumed terrifying proportions.

There were the normal hazards of a deep penetration into the Ruhr Valley. The squadron's bold low-flying technique practised over many weeks might reduce these a little, but even this was problematic. The special danger lay in the form of attack. It was not the object to attempt to breach the Mohne Dam – or the Eder, for that matter – by means of a direct hit. No bomb yet evolved would come anywhere near to doing that. The concrete wall was far too thick. But it was known that concrete, although strongly resistant to the compression of a direct hit, was vulnerable to the tension caused by shock-waves. The theory propounded by Barnes Wallis was that the bombs, or mines, as he called them, must actually be dropped in the waters of the Mohne lake. The resultant explosion, caged and transmitted by the water, would fling at the concrete wall a succession of shock-waves of irresistible force. The sudden contraction and expansion would crumble the massive concrete structure as a high-pitched note might shatter glass.

That was the theory.

For the crews this meant, first, attacking from low level at a constant speed and height. No evasive action. And worse still, in order to maintain the exact height demanded by the limitations of the bomb, they had to carry two search-lights which, shining downwards on the water, formed a figure of eight when the aircraft levelled off at the required height of sixty feet. Thus the gunners on the parapet of the dam and in the surrounding hills would be presented with a steady and illuminated target.

Even this might be tolerable if several aircraft could attack simultaneously and confuse the defences. But the placing of the mines had to be inch-accurate. The rough approximation of a formation attack was not good enough. Each aircraft must make a lone attack.

It was not expected that any one bomb would breach the dam. The effect of the bombing would be cumulative. The dam wall would be successively weakened by each explosion until the stage was reached when one more well-aimed bomb would collapse it.

What chance was there of surviving an illuminated lone attack against the powerful dam defences? The risk was about equal to a lone torpedo attack in daylight against a capital ship – with the added hazard that the defending gunners would be firing from a stable gun-platform. And for those who survived the defences of the Mohne, the attack on the Eder would follow. To postpone it would mean strengthened defences within a few hours.

So when at last, at eleven o'clock on the night before the attack, with all planning and training completed, the enor-mity of the dangers suddenly hit Gibson, he was instantly convinced that no more than two or three aircraft were likely to come through, and certainly not the leader. His reaction was to sit down at once and compose a detailed operation order. Should the worst happen and none of them get back, at least he would have left a complete record of what they had planned to do.

Exhausted by the weeks of training, tensed by the prolonged strain of responsibility, and shaken by the late realisation of the extreme hazards to be faced, Gibson, conscious of the need to recharge his batteries in sleep, left the operations room to go to bed. But outside he was met by his station commander.

'I'm awfully sorry, Guy – but Nigger's had it. He's just been run over, right outside the camp. He was killed instantly.'

Gibson made no answer. He slowly turned away and went to his bunk. Nigger was gone, and there wasn't even time to grieve over him. Perhaps it was as well. But it was more than the loss of a man's dog. Nigger had become a talisman, a symbol of Gibson's own indestructibility. He was the squadron mascot. The code-word that Gibson was to transmit if the Mohne Dam was successfully breached was 'Nigger'. His violent death now held all the threat of an omen.

An intense loneliness settled over Gibson as he reached his room. His wife was in London doing war work. He did not believe in wives living near operational bases – he had seen too often the pale-faced, red-eyed, brave helplessness when the bad news came through. He hadn't even told his wife that he was flying again. There was no comfort to be had from there. And he knew that in the last analysis the leader stood alone. The loss of Nigger made his solitude absolute.

In the circumstances it was a loss that he could share with no one. Most of the squadron would feel genuine grief, but for the moment they must not be allowed to. It would hardly raise morale. The news of Nigger's death must be suppressed.

His eye fell on the scratch-marks on the door of his room,

which Nigger had made in excited, impatient exuberance. He determined not to think about it. But it was a long time before he put his light off. Thanks to the sleeping pills that had been handed out to all the crews that night he eventually slept.

He awoke next morning to a heavy depression which he could not at first shake off. Then he was caught up in a frenzy of last-minute briefings and preparations, and the loss of Nigger and his own premonitions of mortality were forgotten. Or almost forgotten. Before taking off on the raid he drew his ground NCO, 'Chiefy' Powell, quietly aside and told him about the death of Nigger. 'It's a very bad omen,' he said, 'and I want you to keep it dark. You must promise not to tell anyone. But I want you to do something for me. Will you bury Nigger for me at midnight tonight?'

Only the fraction of a raised eyebrow showed that Powell understood. At midnight Gibson would be over the target.

Gibson and the nine crews who formed the main dam-busting force took off from their base at Scampton in Lincolnshire soon after half-past nine that night, 16 May 1943, under a full moon. A diversionary force of five aircraft took off a few minutes earlier to attack a third dam, the Sorpe, and four others stood by to take off later. At the group headquarters at Grantham, Harris, Cochrane and Barney Wallis waited for news.

Now was the time when the men on the ground became plagued with doubts. Wallis's calculations had been put to every conceivable test, but in the eyes of many the raid remained a wild-cat scheme, touching the realms of fantasy. Even those who believed in Wallis had their misgivings now.

Because of the bright moonlight no other bomber aircraft were operating. They had the entire German defences to themselves. And the hazards of the outward flight had not been overestimated. Although the route had been carefully planned to avoid flak positions, this became almost impossible once they crossed the Rhine and entered the valley of the Ruhr.

They played hide and seek with searchlights and flak emplacements by continually weaving and jinking, sometimes even dodging behind lines of trees. Then they flew smack over the middle of a new airfield unmarked on their charts. The two aircraft in close formation with Gibson were so brightly illuminated by searchlights that he could read the squadron letters on each fuselage. One pilot to the left and in the rear of Gibson was blinded by the searchlights and pulled up to gain control. Losing contact and uncertain of his position he turned to look for a pinpoint and dropped behind. A few moments later he was caught by powerful flak defences and badly hit. His Lancaster plunged downwards, struck the ground and burst into flames. Five seconds later the blazing wreckage disintegrated in a pyrotechnic shower as the mine went off.

The diversionary force, too, was faring badly. Two of the five aircraft had been forced to turn back and two had been shot down. That left only the American McCarthy, the leader. At Scampton a decision was taken to despatch the four reserves.

Meanwhile the eight remaining Lancasters led by Gibson had skirted Dortmund and Hamm and were approaching the hills guarding the Ruhr. They shot over the hill-crests right on track and there beneath them, dark and sleek and opaque, lay the waters of the Mohne.

At once a criss-cross barrage of brightly-coloured light flak festooned the lake in streams of lethal ticker-tape, doubled in apparent intensity by the darting reflections in the still water. And rising ahead of them like a fortress they could see the dam itself, twin-towered like the ramparts of a castle, or twin-funnelled like a battleship, an exact replica of the models they had studied that morning, model-like itself in the unreal moonlight. Shrunk as it was by distance, it still seemed massive and sinister. To Gibson it looked squat and thick and unconquerable.

Circling over the hills on the far side of the lake Gibson called each aircraft in turn and was relieved to get seven replies. So far they had lost only one. It was time to attack. But Gibson hesitated, reluctant to put all the weeks of training and hoping to the test. He called his crew. 'Well, chaps, I suppose we'd better start the ball rolling.' He turned and looked again at the compact structure of the dam, and for a moment doubted whether any weapon so far forged could possibly damage it.

'Hello, all Cooler aircraft. Come in to attack when I tell you. I'll attack first.' Then he remembered Melvyn Young, his deputy leader. 'Hello, Melvyn. Stand by to take control if anything goes wrong.' He banked and turned over the wooded hillside towards the lake.

Scraping the tall trees at the lakeside he brought the Lancaster down low over the water, switching on the two searchlights and holding the nose down until the beams merged in a scurrying figure eight. The coloured lights were pouring at them, from the twin-towered parapet, steady in the centre of Gibson's windscreen, and from the surrounding hills, shrouded in haze. The dam wells, grim and foreboding, stared back at Gibson with an eerie malevolence. He remembered something that he had forgotten since take-off – the premonition, the knowledge even, that he was going to die. In another moment it was going to happen. His face was hot under his microphone mask, suffocating with the sweat of fear. He shouted at Pulford, his flight engineer. 'Leave the throttles open. Stand by to pull me out of the seat and take over if I get hit.' Pulford stared back in astonishment. He had never heard Gibson say anything like that.

The height was right and the speed was right. The needle on the air-speed indicator was steady on the pre-set red line. The clatter of machine-gun fire from the front turret startled him and he gripped the stick more tightly as the golden rain sprinted ahead in a gentle arc, forward and downward towards the parapet.

'Left – a bit more left. Steady. Steady.' His bomb-aimer, oblivious to the flak, was reciting his bombing instructions in a flat voice that reached a little crescendo of excitement of its own. 'Coming up now.'

The wireless operator was firing Verey lights to blind and confuse the defences and there was another clatter from the front guns, but the coloured lights continued to rise towards the cockpit like a flow of electrons, a two-way traffic in steel. Then a wide shutter came up out of the water to fill the windscreen – the wall of the dam, dangerously close.

'Mine gone.'

Gibson pulled up just in time and they shot across the parapet, the tail gunner, Trevor-Roper, gleefully spraying the defending gunners. Then they were clear of the dam and out of range.

'Good show, leader,' said a voice on the R/T. 'Bang on.'

A great column of whiteness rose a thousand feet into the air where Gibson's mine had exploded and the tormented water was writhing and seething and splashing over the parapet as though some monster of the lake were thrashing about in its death-throes. At first Gibson thought the dam had gone, but as the great column of water showered back into the lake he saw that it was still intact. Keenly disappointed, he hoped that the powerful and invisible undercurrents were doing their work.

Even when the great maelstrom had subsided it left the water thrashing and turgid, far too disturbed for another mine to be dropped for several minutes. One of the requirements was that each mine must be dropped in calm water.

When the lake at last subsided Gibson called Hopgood, the man briefed to attack second. 'Hello, Hoppy. Attack now. Good luck.'

The men Gibson chose to accompany him on the dambusting raid have achieved immortality. Hopgood has been described by Gibson as the ideal squadron type, fundamentally steady and serious but a good mixer. Fair-haired and of medium height, he was averagely good-looking and might have passed unnoticed but for a single prominent tooth, slightly askew, which lit up his personality. Now Hopgood replied to Gibson in his usual casual manner.

'OK, leader. Attacking now.'

Although Gibson's approach had been seen, the manner of his attack had been novel and it had achieved a measure of surprise. But not so Hopgood's. The ground gunners knew the direction of attack and they recognised the tactics. All they had to do was put down a curtain of fire in front of the charging Lancaster and it had to fly through it.

Gibson watched Hopgood's twin searchlight beams hit and sweep the water. The ground gunners saw them too. From one of the watching aircraft there was a hoarse shout on the R/T.

'Hell, he's been hit.'

A banner of flame was streaking back from the Lancaster's port wing, attracting the flak like moths to a candle. Still the aircraft plunged on, at the right speed and height, until it seemed about to crash into the parapet. Then the mine dropped away and it pulled up. Gibson saw the mine fall. It overshot and fell on a power-house on the far side of the dam, while the aircraft staggered on, clawing for height so that the crew could bale out. But when it reached 500 feet there was a crimson flash, the port wing slowly came away, and the rest of the aircraft plunged earthwards like a meteor, disintegrating as it went.

Someone broke the silence on the R/T. 'Poor old Hoppy.' For Gibson it was not merely the end of his oldest friend on 617, the man who had taught him to fly Lancasters and with whom he had shared the whole of his second bombing tour. It was the end of any chance of success for the operation – unless he could do something quickly about it. Short of some kind of distraction for the defences, the whole squadron would be picked off one by one.

'Let's go in and murder those gunners,' shouted Trevor-Roper. This was the right spirit, but it could only have the same result. Nevertheless an idea was forming in Gibson's mind.

At that moment the yellow moonlight glowed ochreous as Hopgood's mine went off behind the power-house, sending up a vast pall of smoke which poured back across the parapet and into the dam basin. They would have to wait for that to clear.

If Gibson had decided that his chances of surviving the raid were infinitesimal, they must now have seemed to vanish altogether. Because his remedy for the destruction threatened by the loss of Hopgood was for his own aircraft to act as a decoy in all subsequent attacks. He would fly up and down in front of the German gunners with his searchlights playing, deliberately drawing their fire.

He called the next man, Martin. 'OK, Mickey. In you go.'

'OK, leader. Going in now.'

'I'll run in beside you and try to draw off the flak.'

'Thanks, leader.'

Cheshire later described Martin as the greatest operational pilot that the RAF has ever produced, superior even to Gibson. His crew were of the same calibre and included the squadron navigational officer, the gunnery leader, and an expert bomb-aimer. As Martin turned clear of the hills and raced across the lake at 230 miles an hour, Gibson ran in beside him and a little in front. When they came within machine-gun range Gibson turned parallel with the dam and his gunners sprayed the gun positions on the parapet, giving vent to their furious rage at the loss of Hopgood. Even so Martin's aircraft was badly hit on the final run in.

The mine fell accurately and there was the same huge submarine explosion and the same great stalagmite of water escaping skywards. 'OK, leader, attack completed,' called Martin, his crew busily checking to see what damage had been done. There was a large hole in the starboard wing but by good luck the petrol tanks on that side had already been emptied.

As Gibson watched the boiling turmoil of water pounding into the parapet he thought for a moment that the dam wall had moved. But when he looked more closely it seemed as rock-like as ever. If Wallis's calculations had been correct it should surely have cracked by now.

With a sick feeling Gibson ordered the next aircraft in. Was there some unsuspected flaw in Wallis's theory? Was the sacrifice going to be in vain?

One by one, like animals from their lair, the Lancasters emerged from their hiding-place in the surrounding hills on Gibson's call. The next was piloted by Melvyn Young, 'Dinghy' Young because of his partiality for ditching his aircraft (he had done it twice). Born in California, educated at Cambridge, he was Gibson's senior flight commander and a highly efficient organiser, besides being the fastest quaffer of a pint of beer Gibson had ever seen.

'Look out for the flak,' called Gibson. 'It's pretty hot.'

'OK.'

'We'll make a dummy attack from the far side of the parapet this time,' called Gibson. 'My gunners will beat them up and that should give you a clear run.'

'Thanks, leader.'

So here was Gibson again, deliberately simulating his third attack on the dam in order to draw the defensive fire. And the ground gunners fell for the bait. As Young flicked on his twin beams and slid across the lake as though on skis, Gibson was keeping the defenders of the dam busy and frustrated by flying with his identification lights on at the limit of range on the far side and twisting to and fro as though about to attack. Young, subjected only to desultory fire from the hills overlooking the dam, dropped his mine right on the spot. A great tidal wave of water slopped over the dam and down past the power station into the valley.

'I've done it! I think I've done it! It's gone!'

But Young's hoarse excitement was premature. From the far side of the parapet Gibson could see that the dam was still intact.

Four aircraft had now dropped their mines with spectacular results but without apparently weakening the dam. Gibson's wireless operator radioed the news back to Grantham, where Harris and Cochrane were pacing up and down, for once making no effort to conceal their feelings. Barnes Wallis sat with his head in his hands. To him the raid had always been just another experiment – impersonal as the drawing-board, the wind-tunnel, the test-bench. The sudden realisation that brave young men were dying to prove his theories had had a shattering effect on him.

But in Gibson a new excitement was growing, a re-birth, a re-creation, a certainty that he and his squadron were on the brink of success and that he would live to witness it. The mighty wall of the dam still lay there as formidable as ever, bathed in moonlight, apparently indestructible. Yet an indefinable sixth sense seemed to tell him that the structure of the dam had moved, that the concrete wall was wilting under the impact of powerful unseen blows below the surface, that compared with the forces unleashed by the Wallis bomb it was a cardboard edifice, as vulnerable as a stage prop. When he called the next Lancaster in, it was with a new confidence that all the waiting crews recognised.

'OK, No. 5 – attack now. I think it'll go this time.'

A few seconds later David Maltby in the fifth Lancaster emerged from the hills. Maltby was just twenty-one, married and with his wife living out near Scampton. He had been afraid that the dam would be breached before his own turn came. Now he had his chance. For Gibson, aware that he couldn't work the same ruse twice, and coming in this time obliquely across the lake to draw the fire, it was like seeing the same show from a different seat. Martin too was acting as a decoy now.

Maltby's attack was as accurate as those that had gone before; there was the same flak, the same explosion, the same stalagmite of water. But this time Gibson was over the lake and his view was obscured by the tumbling cascade. The whole area around the dam was misty with suspended moisture and spray and Gibson's windscreen was gossamered as though in light rain.

As the water subsided Gibson could see that the dam was still unscathed. Again his mood changed. Sweating with frustration and sick at heart he ordered in the sixth Lancaster.

Dave Shannon, the pilot, crept down across the treetops of the hillside towards the lake, and Gibson turned until he was almost directly above the dam. The scene below flashed and flickered as in a mirage, and he blinked and looked again. Then he heard a shout on the R/T, echoed by many others.

'I think she's gone !'

'It's gone ! Look, the dam's gone !'

A stretch of the dam wall a hundred yards long lay crumpled and smashed and a wide treacly tongue of liquid edged with froth gushed out and over and down, flinging aside the power-house and racing with inexorable purpose towards the industrial centres that the dam had helped to sustain. All the tempestuous agony of the lake had ceased and the stormy surface had smoothed again into glass, satisfied in this one immense blood-letting.

Gibson ordered Shannon to call off his attack and stand by, while the R/T burst into a cacophony of hysteria as the crews shouted at each other in frenzied triumph. They'd done it ! Old Barnes Wallis and his bomb had done it ! The Mohne Dam had been breached.

'Get a message out to group !' exulted Gibson to his wireless operator. 'Nigger ! Nigger ! Nigger !'

Nigger was dead, but, like the crews who would not return, he was immortalised in this greatest air strike of all time. At Grantham, Harris, Cochrane and Wallis were jubilant.

Gibson looked again at the dam and the water. Later, in his book, he described the scene.

'It was the most amazing sight. The whole valley was beginning to fill with fog from the steam of the gushing water and down in the foggy valley we saw cars speeding along the roads in front of this great wave of water which was chasing them and going faster than they could ever hope to go. I saw their headlights burning and I saw the water overtake them, wave by wave, and then the colour of the headlights underneath the water changing from light blue to green, from green to dark purple, until there was no longer anything except the water bouncing down in great waves. The floods raced on, carrying with them as they went, viaducts, railways, bridges, and everything that stood in their path. Three miles beyond the dam the remains of Hoppy's aircraft were still burning gently, a dull red glow on the ground. Hoppy had been avenged.

'I knew that this was the heart of Germany, and the heart of her industries, the place which itself had unleashed so much misery upon the whole world.

'It was a catastrophe for Germany.

'I circled round for about three minutes, then called up all aircraft and told Mickey and David Maltby to go home and the rest to follow me to Eder, where we would try to repeat the performance.'

An hour later, in spite of further tragic losses, the Eder dam, too, was breached. Four of Gibson's main force of nine – Hopgood, 'Dinghy' Young, Astell, and Maudslay – failed to return. And of the seven aircraft which eventually took part in the diversionary and backing-up operations, only three got back. Eight lost out of sixteen, fifty per cent. But the Mohne and the Eder dams were gone. And Gibson himself had miraculously survived.

\*     \*     \*

They took Gibson off operational flying after this. He had done enough, more than enough. And to make it easier for him they sent him with Winston Churchill on a mission to America. It was Churchill who christened him 'dam-buster', and called him nothing else.

His admiration for Churchill turned his mind towards politics. What had he been fighting for? His ideas were not much different from the average Service-man of his time. An end to the inequalities of the thirties. A fresh start. Freedom for the individual. A chance for everyone. He had not been a career man in the Service and he looked beyond it for his future. He agreed to be put up for nomination as prospective Conservative candidate for Macclesfield.

From a distinguished list of possibles Macclesfield chose him. But now he saw that his immediate future was bound up inextricably with the war. He thanked Macclesfield for the honour but declined it. He could not change course until the war was over.

He soon became impatient with the desk job he was given at the Air Ministry, impatient too with the Staff College Wartime Course on which he was subsequently sent. It was during this period that he wrote *Enemy Coast Ahead*, from which many of the facts in this story are taken. It is the best of all the personal bomber stories. But in the meantime the bombing of Germany had reached its zenith and he was itching to play his part.

Now for the first time he clashed with his seniors. Yes, he could continue to contribute to the bomber offensive – but from the ground. A staff job at his old group headquarters was all they would offer him. To all his pleadings for just a few more operational sorties they resolutely turned a deaf ear. It seemed foolish to risk a man of Gibson's calibre and experience on routine bomber operations at this stage of the war.

And Gibson for the first time in his life knew the meaning of suffering. Fear, staleness, fatigue, mental exhaustion – all these things he had beaten. Now the certainty of a prolonged, indefinite rest from operational flying defeated him. He was being denied his whole reason for existence. Three years planning and training for it, four years doing it. He had done nothing else since leaving school. Without the thrill and excitement of intrusion over enemy territory, the comradeship of his fellow air-crews, the loyalty of the ground crews, the daily stimulus of danger, life for him had become intolerable.

One day soon after joining the group staff he was found in his office with tears in his eyes, heart-broken at being separated from his beloved crews. The news got back to Cochrane and Harris and they relented to the extent of posting him to an operational base – Coningsby – where he could breathe and exhale the atmosphere of the bomber offensive although his own personal participation remained strictly forbidden. This posting was perhaps a mistake. It was like forbidding a son to go on the stage and then giving him free tickets for nightly performances. Not surprisingly it aggravated the malady.

Gibson's discontent was intensified one morning in July 1944 when a Mosquito landed at Coningsby. The pilot was his old 617 friend Mickey Martin, now on intruder night fighters. Martin took Gibson up and showed him how to fly the Mosquito. When they landed Gibson spoke his resolve. 'I'm sick of flying a desk. Somehow I've got to get back on ops.'

In desperation he turned to the one man above all others whom he felt would understand – 'Bomber' Harris. It was Harris who had been his group commander on his first tour of operations. It was Harris to whom he had gone when on rest at a fighter training unit with a successful plea to be put back on ops (Harris had then just been made C.-in-C. Bomber Command). It was Harris who had given him the chance, at the conclusion of his second bombing tour, of 'just one more raid'. And now, hungry for the ephemeral but extroverted life of the operational pilot, it was to Harris that he went.

Harris, quite wrongly according to his own admission, gave in. Yet perhaps the time had come when even so powerful a character as Harris could no longer deny Gibson his destiny.

Harris agreed that Gibson should fly on just one more raid. But he instructed Cochrane that the target selected must be close to the Allied lines, not deep in enemy territory. The raid eventually chosen was a medium-sized attack on München Gladbach and the adjacent town of Rheydt, near the west German border. Gibson's aircraft would be a Mosquito, his role that of master bomber, the technique of which he had been the creator and originator in the attack on the dams.

The raid was a part of the incessant attack on communications behind the enemy lines. Two important railway lines, one coming from Aachen to the south-west and the other from Cologne to the south-east, met at Rheydt before running a further two miles north into Munchen Gladbach, where they connected with the main route from the Ruhr into Holland. Important area targets included railway yards, engineering works, and factories making rail components. Three aiming points were chosen, a force of 220 Lancasters being apportioned equally between them. Nine Mosquitoes would mark the targets, three for each aiming point, and a tenth would be flown by the master bomber.

The raid had an unpleasant beginning. Electrical storms and thunder-cloud on the route out set up a dangerous turbulence and the Lancasters were thrown all over the sky. Many crews kept their identification lights on to reduce the collision risk. Most of them were hampered by icing. But near the target the weather cleared and conditions were good except for industrial haze.

The technique of target illumination and marking had reached a high stage of sophistication by this time of the war. But experience showed that the smallest errors in marking and bombing quickly accumulated as bomber after bomber was misled into dropping inaccurately, so that the whole focus of an attack could shift in minutes, perhaps to some scattered area or even into open country. The function of the master bomber was to hold the skeins of the pattern in place, to issue orders for the correction of errors and to call for re-marking where this was necessary. To do this he had to position himself over the target soon after the first flares went down and circle amongst the flak and falling bombs until the raid was over.

This was the task that Guy Gibson had chosen for himself in his first operational flight since May 1943.

The whole raid was planned to the minute. At half-past nine the illuminators were over the target and three minutes later the first flares went down. In the light of them almost the whole of Munchen Gladbach and Rheydt, roads, railways, bridges, buildings, were clearly visible. Then came the markers. The three aiming points were to be marked in different colours – green, red and yellow. The green aiming point was the industrial centre of Munchen Gladbach to the north. The red was the industrial centre of Rheydt to the south. The yellow was the railway junction south of Munchen Gladbach, roughly bisecting the other two aiming points.

The most difficult target to mark was the railway junction, and Gibson called for this to be marked first, before the smoke from other markers impaired visibility. The marker for the Yellow Force dived from 3000 feet to 800 and dropped his target indicators right on the junction. Gibson, circling overhead, applauded his accuracy and called in the two backers-up. There was no problem here. Then he called in the marker for the Green Force. Some of the flares had gone down slightly south and east of Munchen Gladbach, so that the centre of the town was not so well illuminated. Gibson pointed this out and warned the marker to place his indicators in the middle of the industrial area. The marker Mosquito dived from 2000 feet to 700 and dropped his indicator accurately but it disappeared through a roof. Gibson called in the two backers-up. By a quarter to ten the northern aiming point was fairly well marked, though the target indicators were slightly offset to the west. Gibson called in the Green Force to drop their bombs, warning them to overshoot by 200 yards.

Meanwhile he had asked for the marker for the Red Force, but here there was a delay. On his way to the target the pilot had noticed that the exhaust stub on the port side of his Mosquito had worked loose. He decided to feather the engine, but this cut down his speed so much that he realised he would be late over the aiming point. The Red

Force bombers would be left circling in confusion. He restarted the port engine and caught up on his schedule, but when he dived down to plant his target indicator the stub blew off and the glare from the exposed exhaust blinded him. He could not drop his indicator.

The success of the raid now depended on the master bomber. The crews of the Red Force would not wait for long. It was too unhealthy. They would drop their bombs indiscriminately and get clear of the target area. Two or three of them had already done just that. Other crews would come in and bomb the resultant fires and the whole focus of the attack would shift.

Gibson called the Red Force. 'Stand by, Main Red Force. Do not bomb.'

But he could not keep them circling indefinitely. A minute later there were still no red indicators. 'OK, Red Force,' called Gibson, 'come in and bomb the green markers.' It was hard luck on Munchen Gladbach and good luck for Rheydt, but it would keep the bombing concentrated until the red markers went down.

Positioning himself for a second dive at the red aiming point, this time on one engine, the red marker marked the target successfully at nine-fifty and the backers-up followed. At once Gibson cancelled his previous orders and instructed the Red Force to bomb the red target indicators as originally briefed.

Gibson then sent the markers home, and the raid settled down to its planned pattern, with no time and very few bombs wasted. In spite of strong flak defences and the continual depredations of night fighters, who dropped their own flares and several times threw Gibson's circling Mosquito into silhouette thousands of feet below the bomber force, the attack proved highly successful and achieved its triple objects. Twenty minutes after the dropping of the first illuminator the last bomb went down.

'OK, chaps,' called Gibson, 'nice work. Now beat it home.'

It seems that for Gibson, and for his navigator, Squadron

Leader J. B. Warwick, these words may have had a wistful ring. Gibson's Mosquito had been hit.

Forty-five minutes later, it was the rough running of Gibson's engines that riveted the attention of Anton de Bruyn, the night watchman at the sugar factory at Steenbergen. It was Gibson's Mosquito that was circling the town.

Suddenly the engines coughed. The crash of a crippled bomber was a frequent occurrence over the Low Countries, but it had never before come to the quiet backwater of Steenbergen. For a moment, as people all over the town threw up their windows and looked out, there was silence. Then they saw the jet of flame, the steep arc towards the ground. For some there was a last view of two hunched figures silhouetted against the fire on the far side of the aircraft, and then came the dreaded crash and explosion.

The good people of Steenbergen hurried to the scene. The Mosquito had been totally destroyed on impact and the two bodies thrown out. Both were mutilated and unrecognisable. The remains were carefully gathered together and placed in a single coffin. All the documents found in the plane were quickly hidden in the Town Hall.

An identity disc marked 'J. B. Warwick' was found, also an envelope addressed 'Squadron Leader J. B. Warwick, DFC, RAF Coningsby'. So one member of the crew was positively identified. The only clue to the identity of the second crew member was a tiny white tab sewn into a charred sock on which was inscribed the name 'Gibson'. No one guessed that the sock belonged to Guy Gibson, VC.

Steenbergen was not far from the Allied lines and the Nazi mayor had already fled. The deputy mayor, a loyal Dutchman, in touch with the mood of the people, decided to give the two fliers a ceremonial burial, with a cortège led by members of the Civil Defence in uniform. But the local German commandant, hearing of the plan next morning, ordered an immediate burial within the hour, so the procession had to be abandoned.

This did not prevent the people of Steenbergen from honouring the crew of the Mosquito with a worthy burial. The coffin was put on a funeral car and covered with the flag of the Netherlands, and the cortège was followed by the deputy mayor and other civic dignitaries as well as the Pastor and a Roman Catholic priest. To the annoyance of the occupation troops, many of the villagers attended the funeral to give a last salute to the brave airmen whose lives they recognised had been given in the cause of liberation. A single white cross marked the joint grave. On it was stencilled the name of Squadron Leader Warwick. The rest of the cross was left blank, but the unknown airman was none the less revered.

It was not until some months later, after Steenbergen had been liberated, that the War Graves Commission confirmed that the unknown airman was none other than Wing Commander Guy Gibson, VC, DSO, DFC, greatest of all bomber pilots. He had earlier been reported missing from the raid of 19 September 1944, and later missing presumed dead. His name was then written, sadly but with pride, on the slender white cross that marked his grave.

For those who reproached themselves bitterly for allowing Gibson to take part in one more raid there was the consolation that the German night skies had been his element, an element in the creation of which he had played a decisive and perhaps the leading part, but an element which with the war's end must pass out of human experience. The whole convoluted technique of aerial bombardment as developed in the last two years of the war had grown from Gibson's original leadership of the raid on the dams. His contribution to victory was incalculable.

# 7

## 'Jacko'

Fʀᴇᴅ Mɪꜰꜰʟɪɴ, twenty-two-year-old pilot from Newfound-land, tall, fair and powerfully built, switched on his microphone and called 'Sandy' Sandelands, his dark-haired, plumpish wireless operator, on the inter-com. 'Keep a look-out for a blip on the radar, Sandy. Let me know if you see anything.'

'Roger.' Sandelands was staring into Fishpond, the tiny screen which reflected the image of any aircraft picked up by the questing radar impulses. Usually on a big raid he saw scores of images, mostly of friendly aircraft in the bomber stream. Tonight he blinked and stared and manipulated his controls continually and yet saw nothing.

Twenty-thousand feet below them lay the smouldering ruin of Schweinfurt, Central Germany, fifty miles north-west of Nuremberg. But as they approached the target area, everything was strangely, ominously quiet. A lone Lancaster, last over the target, they were being given a clear run by the ground defences. There were no searchlights, there was no flak. This could have only one meaning. There must be night-fighters about, probably one particular fighter, being vectored from the ground at this moment, perhaps already fixing them on its radar, boring in for the kill.

They had started out in the last wave. But because of a following wind they had got ahead of their scheduled time over the target and had dog-legged for the last hundred miles. The other crews, it seemed, hadn't been so particular. Left behind, they had lost the protection of the bomber stream.

There had been an atmosphere of suppressed excitement

and expectancy tonight amongst the whole crew, right from the start. They were on the last sortie of their tour, and they had felt like schoolboys breaking up. After this trip there would be a short leave and then a transfer to the Pathfinder Force. The whole crew had volunteered, preferring to continue in partnership on operations rather than scatter to various conversion and training units. They would never have the confidence in strangers that they had developed in each other.

Like most crews they had come through a good many vicissitudes together, right from their training days. The shy, youthful Mifflin, who hardly knew what it was to drink or smoke, had had no part in the original selection of the crew. Some of the others, getting together and then looking around for a pilot, had liked the look of him and grabbed him. But Mifflin – or 'Miff' as he soon came to be known – wonderful pilot though he proved himself to be, had one weakness. Immensely strong, he was inclined to be heavy-handed at the controls, and he couldn't put a Lancaster down without bouncing it. The crew got used to it, and loved it as an idiosyncrasy, even when it resulted – as it sometimes did – in personal injury. Instructors and flight commanders took a different view. They tried to put Mifflin back for further training, transferring his crew to another pilot, and at one stage they even talked of taking him off flying altogether. But the crew obstinately insisted on sticking together : and Mifflin's other qualities were so obvious and his general popularity so great that in the end they were left alone. Later, when they got to 106 Squadron, and Hugh Johnson, the tail gunner, was injured in a heavy landing and off flying for two months as a result, the crew refused to accept a permanent replacement, and when Johnson was fit he saw to it that he got in several extra bombing trips with another crew to catch up with his own.

Such solidarity was bound to pay dividends in the air. They always stuck rigidly to 'the drill' – not necessarily to the regulations, often it was a peculiar drill evolved by themselves – but each man knew exactly what was expected of him, normally and in emergency. They achieved a similar relationship with their ground crew – six men who took an immense pride in the aircraft and its exploits and who were encouraged to feel an integral part of a thirteen-man crew.

And so to Schweinfurt, and the thirtieth and last trip of their tour. Indeed for Norman Jackson, 'Jacko', the black-haired, self-assured fitter turned flight-engineer, the trip was actually his thirty-first. He had stood in for someone else one night and got ahead of the rest of his crew. He was doing this trip for luck, to see his friends safely through.

Just before take-off he had received the news of the birth of his son. It was his first child, but he meant to have a large family. Alma, his wife, felt the same way. They planned to have four or five children, possibly six or seven. An adopted child himself, 'Jacko' understood and valued the unity and companionship of family life. Now at least he had made a start.

He stood next to Mifflin as they began the bombing run, watching the engine instruments intently. Those four Merlin engines were his special charge. Going into action, though, he was the spare man, ready to take over any job in the aircraft, even the pilot's, if someone should get knocked out. Provided of course that the engines kept going. They remained his first concern.

There was something eerie about the target's passivity, as though all human life in the city below had been obliterated. Yet every man in the crew was apprehensive – much more so than usual. While the wireless operator watched his bowl for signs of fish, the three gunners, front, upper and rear, peered helplessly into the black opaqueness outside. 'Jacko' put his head into the blister window that protruded into the slipstream on his right, but still there was nothing to see. Perhaps the fighters had packed up and gone home.

Maurice Toft, the bomb-aimer, came out of the front turret and crouched over his bomb-sight in the nose compartment, passing his instructions back to Mifflin on the inter-com. They went in and dropped their bombs, aiming at the fierce fires still burning in the centre of the town. Isolated bursts of flak, eruptions from a spent pyrotechnic, spun lazily skywards. A single searchlight traced a swift arc across the heavens and then flickered out. The show was over.

They turned, began a detour to avoid flying back over the city, and set course for home.

'I've got a blip,' called Sandelands.

'What is it?'

'Can't tell. About a thousand yards astern.'

'Probably another Lancaster.'

'We'll soon know.'

Mifflin called Johnson, the rear gunner. 'Did you get that, Johnny? There's an aircraft on Fishpond, a thousand yards astern. Any sign?'

'Not a thing. I'll watch out.' Johnson, taller and younger even than his skipper, the fine bone structure of his face suggesting an aesthetism unusual in a gunner, stared down into the impenetrable blackness, waiting for the fighter to spring at him. He knew that all too often the first the tail gunner knew was the burst that killed him or shot him down.

'Eight hundred yards,' called Sandelands. 'He's closing.'

'It's a fighter all right,' said Mifflin. Another Lancaster would never have closed the distance so quickly. He began corkscrewing, trying to confuse the enemy pilot. This was the recommended manoeuvre against the German airborne radar. So far the Lancaster could be no more than a blip on the German's radar screen.

Johnson, narrowing his eyes in the darkness, caught a glimpse of something metallic climbing up from below, hurtling straight at him. 'Dive!' he shouted. 'Dive starboard!'

It was an FW 190. Johnson got in a single burst, and so did Toft, now back in the front turret, and the mid-upper gunner, 'Smudger' Smith. Mifflin thrust the stick forward but in the same moment the Lancaster was raked by cannon and machine-gun fire. No one was hit, but 'Jacko', the only man not strapped into a seat, was thrown to the floor. Struggling across to the blister, he was just in time to see the FW 190 breaking away. He was aware, too, of something more. The engine immediately below him – the starboard inner – was on fire.

The fire seemed to be right inside the engine. On the dashboard in front of him was a button that operated an extinguisher in the engine itself. He pressed it and the fire lessened considerably. But a few moments later, when he looked again, the flame had grown as strong as ever. He operated the extinguisher button again and again, but now it made no difference. The fire was gaining a hold.

It could be only a matter of minutes before the fire reached the petrol tank on the upper surface of the wing and the aircraft blew up. He had to do something at once. Fortunately they seemed to have shaken off the fighter.

He spoke to his skipper. 'I think I can deal with it, Fred.'

'What can you do?'

He pointed to the roof hatch behind him. 'I'm going to climb out on to the wing with a fire extinguisher. If I can force the nozzle inside the engine cowling I'll soon fix that fire.'

Mifflin looked incredulously at Jackson for a moment, and then accepted the suggestion without comment, so absolutely sure of himself did Jackson seem.

'All right.' Meanwhile he gave the order to the rest of the crew to stand by to bale out, in case Jackson should fail.

Jackson had discussed the feasibility of climbing out on to the wing of a Lancaster in flight many times, mostly with Maurice Toft. It was something that had never been done, although someone had once climbed out on to the wing of a Wellington by kicking footholds in the geodetic construction. That wasn't possible in a Lancaster.

He called to Toft and his navigator, Frank Higgins. 'Come and give me a hand.' But the inter-com had now gone dead.

Jackson had considered the dangers and he was ready for them. He would need his parachute, in case he fell off the wing – or in case he couldn't get back. He hadn't really worked out that part of it yet – it would have to wait. He figured that the safest thing to do was to pull his parachute inside the fuselage, before he left the aircraft. Then Toft and Higgins could help steady him by holding on to the rigging lines. If he fell off or was blown off, they would never be able to haul him back, but they could pay out the lines and then the canopy and he would be able to descend safely.

To Jackson it was all quite simple and straightforward, nothing particularly daring, just another job of work for which he was responsible and which he was quite capable of doing. He had the same confidence in Toft and Higgins, in whose hands his life would almost certainly rest.

He unclipped a hand fire-extinguisher from the fuselage and thrust it firmly into his battle-dress jacket, where it was securely held beneath his harness and Mae West. He clipped his parachute on to his harness and climbed up on to the navigation table. Above him, and slightly to the rear of the cockpit, was the astro hatch.

Now to spill his parachute. He jerked the ripcord, and at once was almost choked in rigging lines and silk. Toft, scrambling up into the cockpit from the nose to report that he had opened the forward escape hatch, found his way barred by a billowing mass of white froth tinged with red as it glowed in the flame from the wing. He grabbed armfuls of canopy and gathered them against his chest as he crawled up the steps into the cockpit. There he glimpsed Mifflin heaving at the controls, trying to keep the damaged Lancaster straight and level, and Jackson reaching up towards the astro hatch, apparently about to bale out. Thinking that Jackson had pulled his 'chute by mistake, he began to pass the folds he had gathered up towards him, but Jackson waved the tangled mass of silk away, pointing first at the hatch and then at the wing, and giving him the 'thumbs-up' signal. Mifflin, too, was giving the same signal, evidently satisfied that he could hold the Lancaster steady, and Jackson's intention was now clear.

Toft and Higgins gathered the canopy into folds and stowed it safely, and then grabbed the rigging lines and pulled in the slack until they were as taut as a harness. Now to jettison the hatch. Jackson pulled the lever, and the violence of the down-draught knocked him backwards so that he almost fell off the table. Recovering his balance, he reached upwards and secured a hold with both hands, one on each side of the hatch.

He levered his body up on his hands and wrists until he was able to swing his elbows out and rest his weight on them, first one and then the other. Now, with his head bent into the slipstream, he peered out over the fuselage and down below him and slightly aft to the wing.

The icy cold blast of the 200-mile-an-hour slipstream struck him like a heavy blow in the chest, penetrating his clothing so that he felt naked, and freezing his throat and nostrils so that his lungs cried out. For a moment he gasped for breath. Above him a ceiling of stars danced like myriads of tiny lanterns, incredibly close, while the great bowl of space seemed to lie below him, dark and limitless and unfathomable. Recovering his breath, he focused again on the wing.

The fire in the engine was still burning fiercely below him. He climbed clear of the hatch, still holding on tightly, his body curled back along the top of the fuselage, wrestling with the slipstream as with a live enemy. With the fingers of his left hand still curled tightly over the lip of the hatch, he began to work his body into position prior to dropping down on to the wing.

Retaining his grip, he lowered his body slowly down the side of the fuselage towards the wing. Buffeted in the slipstream, he dare not let go of the hatch.

His feet touched metal and he stood firmly on the wing. Still his only hold was the lip of the hatch. In a moment he would have to transfer his grip from the hatch to the wing, and he looked for a likely hold. Just ahead of him, at the leading edge of the wing, between the fuselage and the blazing engine, was the air intake. If he could get a grip on that he would be ideally placed to deal with the engine. He would have to push hard forward against the slipstream, let go above, fall flat on the wing, and grab.

Whichever way he attempted it, there would be a period of a full second in which he had no grip at all.

There was no sense in hesitating. Throwing his weight hard forward, he let go.

The wind struck him a fearful blow and as he hurled himself forward he slipped. Precious inches of the wing swept by underneath him. He ducked his head down and snatched desperately at the air intake. He felt his finger-nails tearing on metal. Then he felt the opening of the air intake and his fingers slotted into it like a clamp. The tug loosened his armpits, but his grip held.

Stretched out full length on the wing, his head level with the leading edge, he could almost touch the flames escaping from the engine. There was a small opening in the cowling on this side, just above the exhaust pipe, and through it he could see the fire raging.

Strengthening his grip with his left hand, he relaxed his right slowly and then let go. Satisfied, he brought it back slowly towards the extinguisher. He eased the extinguisher out of his harness, gripped it, lifted it up against the slipstream, and knocked the nozzle off on the wing. One sharp tap and it began hissing. Then the jet flowed. He thrust it at once into the opening in the cowling. The fire began to die down.

The jet went on spewing into the engine. The fire had stopped. He was winning.

In a moment or two the jet would be spent and he would be free to climb back. But how was he going to manage it?

All his plans for this operation had concerned getting out on to the wing and holding on. Now he could see that this was only half the problem, and the easy half at that. A much more difficult problem was getting back. Throwing his body forward and down and grabbing the air intake had been one thing. But how could he get the impetus for an upward grab at the hatch.

Once he let go of the air intake he would have nothing to grip. The slipstream would sweep him off the wing instantly. He wondered if he might manage to get a foothold in the air intake and climb up from there. But changing his grip would involve precarious moments. And if he fell forward of the wing, what would happen to his parachute? Almost certainly it would be blown back towards the tail. Even if his free-falling weight dragged it forward again it would be torn to shreds by the propellers.

Suddenly he felt the plane bank to port. He clung on grimly, wondering what on earth they were doing. Then he knew. The fighter had found them again. He heard the stutter of machine-gun fire and felt stabs of pain in his back and legs. The next moment the fire-extinguisher was torn from his grasp and the engine burst into a mass of flame which all but enveloped him.

He felt his fingers relaxing their grip on the air intake and he was powerless to tighten it. He tried to regain his grip with his right hand but the muscles would not answer. For a moment his body slid backwards along the wing. Then an inexorable force grabbed him roughly and flung him backwards into space.

He saw the tail unit of the Lancaster shoot past, then felt his body caught and held as though in a net. Now he was being dragged along at 200 miles an hour, the tail turret of the Lancaster only a few yards in front of him, utterly unattainable.

The rigging lines of his parachute, ignited by the explosion in the engine and scorched by the blow-back of flames from the blazing wing, were fraying and smouldering above him. Soon the lines would snap and his last tenuous hold on life would be gone.

What was happening inside the aircraft?

Below the hatch, Higgins and Toft were working desperately to free the parachute canopy and push it out of the hatch before baling out themselves. At any moment the Lancaster would blow up.

'He must have had it,' shouted Toft, 'yet he might be still all right. We've got to get this out.' Their main concern was to keep the canopy free from obstructions as the weight of Jackson's body began to tug it out, but several times a panel fouled a piece of metal and ripped clean across.

The Lancaster was losing speed, diving and lurching to the left. As in some fantastic aerial trapeze act, Jackson was dragged round and down in an ever-steepening curve. Then the aircraft seemed to put on a tremendous spurt and leave him hopelessly behind. He couldn't tell whether the rigging lines had snapped or whether Toft and Higgins had finally freed the canopy. For several seconds he dropped like a stone. Then there was a flapping of wings above him and a jerk and tugging at his waist and armpits, and a moment later he was pirouetting giddily downwards in the silent darkness.

The fire in the rigging lines had spread to the canopy, which was smouldering above him, a sword of Damocles ready to cut him adrift. He grasped the rigging lines with both hands and began to drag them down towards him, squeezing them as he did so, leaving them charred but mostly still tensile. As he pulled the canopy down towards him the air spilled out and he felt himself falling more sharply. The canopy was pock-marked with neatly rounded holes, clean but brown at the edges, like cigarette burns in a handkerchief. But the smouldering seemed to have stopped. He released the rigging lines slowly and was relieved to see the canopy billow slightly and check the velocity of his fall.

The pain in his back and legs was severe but so far the feeling had not returned to his hands, on which the skin had shrivelled and contracted in the heat of the flames. He looked down at them abstractedly, bemused but vaguely comprehending. Above him, torn strands of the rigging fluttered untidily and the wind screeched through the singed canopy. He could expect a heavy fall.

The gentle swinging motion of the descent soothed him and acted as a soporific. For a time he tried to control the parachute's gyrations, but he only succeeded in twisting the lines. He gave it up and relaxed. He had no idea of his rate of fall but guessed that it must be dangerously rapid. When at last he saw the dark shadows of earth below him he was astonished at the swiftness of their approach.

When the ground collided with him he hit it awkwardly and with a terrific crack. He lay quite still for a long time, winded and barely conscious. He seemed to be partly buried, and then he realised that he had fallen amongst bushes and scrub, apparently on the edge of a forest. He tried to move but found he was pinned by branches and bracken. Both his ankles seemed to be broken and his flesh was scratched and torn.

He lay still again, seeking a lower plane of consciousness, but his wounds and injuries began a random insistent throb. His left leg ached from the shell splinters, and stabs of pain shot through his ankle when he tried to ease his position. His right ankle was useless. His hands and face had both been severely burned. His right eye seemed to be closed, and his back had stiffened. He began to wonder how far he was from civilisation and whether he would ever be found.

At daybreak he struggled to his knees, elbowed his way clear of the bushes, and crawled painfully forward. Soon he reached a mercifully soft mat of grass. Ahead of him there seemed to be a forest path. Supporting himself on elbows and knees, he dragged himself forward.

Fear of capture had gone. The very word had lost its meaning. All he looked for was succour from some fellow human being. He was getting deeper and deeper into the forest, but he gave no thought to turning back. Progress won as painfully as this could not be surrendered.

He seemed to have crawled for many hours when at last he made out the shape of a cottage adjacent to the path. He knocked on the door with his elbow. He waited a minute, and knocked again. Then he heard the sound of a window opening upstairs. He strained to look up.

'Was ist das?'

'RAF.' His power of enunciation had gone and the words sounded like a grunt. He cleared his throat and tried again. This time he spoke the letters clearly. 'RAF.'

'Churchill gangster!' called the voice. Then the window banged down as though the encounter had ended. But within a minute he could hear the bolts of the door in front of him being shot back, and a middle-aged German stood glowering fiercely above him.

'Terror flieger!' The farmer spat the words at him and he flinched in spite of himself at the expectation of kicks and blows. But as he did so the farmer was suddenly pulled from his gaze like a puppet and two girls took his place.

They were the farmer's daughters, and they bent kindly to question him, then helped him into the cottage and lifted him on to a couch. The farmer watched sullenly. The girls covered him with blankets, dressed his burns, and gave him hot drinks. The farmer disappeared.

This could be only a brief respite. Soon the farmer would return, and with him would come the police. He wondered how far the cottage was from the town.

The farmer was gone a long time. When he came back he brought the Gestapo.

At once the treatment switched from tenderness to cruelty. The town was a long way away. They made him walk there, limping painfully on a badly sprained ankle, dragging a broken one after him, helped by a civilian policeman.

After rough first aid in the local hospital he was paraded through the streets, where he was greeted by jeers and stone-throwing. Too far gone to care, he guessed that only his pitiable condition saved him from rough handling or worse.

Three weeks later the news reached England that Jackson and four other members of the crew were prisoners. Toft, Higgins, Sandelands and Smith had all baled out safely, but

Fred Mifflin and Hugh Johnson were killed. When last seen by the rest of the crew Mifflin had been half-standing at the controls as though about to bale out. It may be that immediately afterwards he lost control and was unable to reach either of the escape hatches, that only his tremendous strength had enabled him to maintain control for so long. Johnson, too, was found in the aircraft, and it may be that one of these two men stayed on to help the other. They were close friends.

The award of the DFC to Mifflin, recommended earlier, came through after he was reported missing.

Jackson spent the next ten months in a German POW hospital and made a good recovery, although his hands would never again be of more than limited use. At his pre-war trade of fitter he was finished. But a man with such faith in himself would find another niche. He found it soon enough – as a salesman and traveller.

When, after the war, Jackson's story was told, it brought the award of the VC. 'I'd be scared to crawl out on to a balcony now,' he admitted later. 'I was young and cocky and thought I could do anything. But I did no more than anyone else would do.'

In fact there is only one other recorded case of anyone climbing out on to a wing of a modern bomber in flight to extinguish a fire, and that, too, was a VC.

# 8

## The Air Cadet

SERGEANT ARTHUR AARON, twenty-one-year-old former Air Training Corps cadet from Leeds, called his crew on the inter-com.

'Look at it. Take a good look at it. You'll probably never see anything like it again as long as you live.'

Aaron was staring enthralled at a picture whose beauty and magnificence were breathtaking. The Alps by moonlight, from 15,000 feet. There was the aloof barrier of the mountain ranges, then the glass pool of Lake Geneva, then the twinkling lights of the town, and towering above them all, even above the aircraft, the pointed turret of Mont Blanc, with its headgear of clouds and snow. It was a scene that no one could ever forget. But to Aaron, staring at it through the port window of his Stirling bomber on the way to Turin, it had a special significance. An architect in embryo, and a bomber pilot by force of circumstances, he hated the monstrous destruction of war. Yet here in the midst of conflict was this reminder of the permanence of a greater architecture. The scene had about it all the timelessness of indestructible things.

Aaron's mother was of Swiss extraction – his grandfather had been pure Swiss. He loved mountains, and had spent many a boyhood holiday in Switzerland, climbing the ranges that now stretched in panorama before him. But the intensity of their beauty had never struck him quite so forcibly as tonight. The night air was crystal clear, and the moonlight sparkled on the snowy summits and threw vertiginous shadows steeper even than the precipitous slopes of the higher peaks. It was a study in black and white, so varied that one could scarcely believe that all the colours of the spectrum were not there. And the scene was further illuminated by the cold light of danger – not acute, nothing more than a single arc-lamp switched on in a brilliantly-lit arena, but giving a heightened sense of perception, like a drug. Yes, tonight was unique. No pair of eyes would ever look at this scene in quite the same light. Remove the danger and the picture would lose that trick of refulgence for which painters were famous. Increase it and the mind wouldn't have the tranquillity to absorb the scene.

They would never have an easier trip than tonight. First the perfect weather and the bright moonlight, greatly reducing the natural hazards of the long flog over the Alps. Then the target, Turin, nothing like so heavily defended as the bigger German towns. And lastly the tactical situation. The Allies had almost completed the rout of the Axis forces in Sicily, and the Northwest African Air Forces were pounding away at roads and railways in Southern Italy. There would be little spare Italian effort for the defence of Turin.

Thursday 12 August 1943. For Aaron and his crew their twenty-first trip, and their first to Italy. They had taken off from their airfield at Downham Market in Stirling 'O for Oboe' at half-past nine that evening. With double summer time it had still been daylight, and the perimeter fence and adjacent roads had been lined with the good Norfolk villagers, waving and wishing them well. Even as they rendezvoused with 150 other Stirlings over London there had still been the warm, dusty evening glow of late summer. Richmond, the mid-upper gunner, also a Yorkshireman, had called the rest of the crew.

'What's that place we're going over?'

'London, you clot.'

'I *thought* it wasn't big enough for York.'

Aaron had joined in the general laughter. His was a high-spirited crew, composed entirely of NCOs, over whom he exercised a youthful but none the less effective control. On the ground he seemed a mild young man – there were some who were deceived into thinking him meek and mild. But his crew knew better. When they first went on operations he applied a strict no-smoking rule in the air, and he also introduced a ban on drink on the day of the operation. Both these rules could be irksome, but they were obeyed. He insisted on each crew-member making a study of at least one job in the aircraft other than his own in case of emergency, and every man was given a chance to learn how to fly the aircraft, in case he himself should be incapacitated. There was no doubt who was boss in the air.

But tonight was almost too good to be true. The order for 'full tanks' had suggested that the target would be Berlin, and briefing for Turin had come as a relief. If there was any apprehension at all in the minds of the crew, it was mostly superstitious in origin. As they climbed to cross the Alps on their way to the target, Thursday 12 August had shaded into Friday the 13th.

The Alps behind them, they ran in towards Turin in a normal approach, descending gradually to 9000 feet for their bombing run. Malcolm Mitchem, the flight engineer from the West Country, came forward from his engineer's panel in the fuselage and sat on Aaron's right in the second pilot's seat. Allan Larden, the strongly-built Canadian bomb-aimer, went down into the nose to operate the bomb-sight. Bill Brennan, the Canadian nagivator, Aaron's closest friend, stayed in his seat and carried on with his job, working out a course to steer away from the target after the drop. Jimmie Guy, the diminutive wireless operator, formerly a bus conductor in Northampton and at thirty-five by far the oldest man in the crew, took up his post below the mid-upper turret to make sure that the photo-flash which they would drop as their bombs fell didn't hang up. The two gunners, Richmond in the mid-upper turret and McCabe in the rear, kept a look-out for fighters, particularly on the 'dark' side, away from the moon. But it was clear that opposition was going to be meagre. Single bursts of flak, distinct as revolver shots, rose from the city, and the probing searchlight fingers could be counted on one hand. Even the night fighters, never very active over Italian cities, would have difficulty in getting within range in that fierce moonlight.

'We'll do our bombing run straight and level,' called Aaron. 'There's no point in weaving.' They might as well make the best of the conditions and drop their bombs as accurately as possible. It was a logical decision, but Aaron noted that he was overtaking a Stirling ahead of him and slightly to the right, which with exaggerated caution was making a normal weave approach.

'Watch that bloke up front, Art,' called Richmond.

'I've got him.'

When they first picked out the other Stirling it had been a mile or more ahead. Now it was no more than a quarter of a mile away and they could pick out its silhouette almost as clearly as in daylight. It was still weaving and soon they would catch it but it was well to the right and there was no danger of collision.

'Bomb-doors open,' called Aaron.

Mitchem leaned forward, head down, grasped the lever and moved it into the open position. As he did so he saw a dozen little coloured lights streaming through the fuselage and passing between his legs under the seat. He had no idea what they were, and they seemed perfectly harmless, but they must be coming from somewhere. He sat up and looked out, and stared straight into the tail turret of the other Stirling, now no more than 250 yards ahead of them. Slowly and methodically the tail gunner of the Stirling was raking them wing-tip to wing-tip with machine-gun fire.

'Some bastard's shooting at us!'

'I'm hit!'

'Fire back at him, Rich!'

'I can't – the wing-tip's in the way.'

'Bill's gone down.'

The inter-com was alive with shouts. The windscreen on the pilot's side was shattered and there was a hail of flying glass. Mitchem, still shielded by the good half of the windscreen, had no idea what damage had been done. Apart from a glancing blow in the ankle he seemed to have escaped injury himself. Meanwhile Aaron was waving his left arm at him and pointing down. He looked up at Aaron to try to divine what he wanted, but there were no lights in the cockpit and the black-out paint over the top of the canopy shut out the moonlight, so that he could not see Aaron's face. He realised that they were turning and diving to the left, and looking at the instrument panel he saw the air speed building up dangerously and the altimeter needle unwinding rapidly. Aaron was still motioning to him with his left arm, but Mitchem's first concern was the engines and he wanted to get back to his panel. Then, as the diving turn brought them round to face the moon, the cockpit was flooded with light and he saw Aaron's face.

'My God, fellows, look at Art. Oh, poor Art.'

Aaron had been hit in the lower jaw, and it seemed to Mitchem, in that eerie but shadowy light, that half his jaw had been shot away. His oxygen mask and microphone had gone, so that he was unable to communicate with anyone even if he was still able to talk. His right arm hung useless at his side, virtually severed at the elbow. He had severe chest wounds. Yet by some freak of chance, or perhaps supreme effort of will, he had remained conscious. Unable to control the plane, he had slumped towards the left of the cockpit in a collapsed state, but was still signalling Mitchem with his good hand to take over.

Mitchem grabbed the control column on his side of the cockpit and pulled back on it as hard as he could. The Stirling was still in a diving turn to port and the speed had built up to around 250. The stick seemed immovable, but he centralised the ailerons and kept pulling back with all his strength until, at about 3000 feet, she slowly came out.

'Bill's had it.' It was Guy on the inter-com, telling them that Brennan, the navigator, was dead. He lay in a crumpled heap on the floor, his pencil, dividers and instruments scattered over his torn and blood-stained Mercator charts, his eyes still open and his chewing gum still between his lips. He had been shot through the heart, killed by a single bullet, one of the bullets that had passed underneath Mitchem in the cockpit.

Larden, kneeling over the bomb-sight in the nose, had had a miraculous escape. Half a dozen little fingerholes had been punched in the fuselage two feet from his head and body, grazing his face and chest and cutting into his parachute harness, but as in some circus knife-throwing act he had escaped serious injury. He came up from the nose and squeezed past Aaron and Mitchem. Aaron was still hunched over to the port side, his face covered with blood and his jaw a gaping wound, and Mitchem was still fighting with the controls. He helped Mitchem pull the Stirling out of the dive and then went back to the fuselage, where he took control, moving the navigator's body to make room for Aaron, and then sitting down at the navigation table to confirm the course out before going forward again.

The momentum of the dive enabled Mitchem to regain much of the lost height. The windscreen on his side was still undamaged, and through it he could see the city in the light of the marker flares, which were still pouring down. He could see bomb explosions and fires and pick out landmarks such as bridges, but he knew it was hopeless to attempt to go in and bomb. The throttle control pedestal had been wrecked, the two inboard engine throttle controls had been shot away so that he could not alter the settings, the starboard outer was losing power and wouldn't answer to the throttle lever, and the only engine he could control was the port outer. He turned on to a reciprocal course, remembering that the turning point on both inward and outward courses had been the lake north of Chambéry, and used the port motor to try to gain height for the mountain crossing. Meanwhile Larden and Guy had half-dragged and half-carried Aaron out of the pilot's seat and back into the fuselage, where they made him as comfortable as they could on the floor against the engineer's panel, putting a parachute under his head. Between them they got a shell dressing on Aaron's face and attended as best they could to his arm, which they put in a sling. Then Larden went forward to take over from Mitchem.

He got into the left-hand seat, but the shattered windscreen in front of him made flying the aircraft even more difficult and unpleasant. The right-hand seat was better, but the weight of the controls imposed a considerable muscular strain in both positions, and the two men took it in turns to fly. It was clear that they would need more height, and Larden went down into the nose to jettison the bomb-load. They were unaware that one of the bombs, a 4000-pounder of a secret type, fused to an unknown delay, had hung up in the bomb-racks.

They began to look for a way through the mountains. In spite of continual manipulation of the remaining throttles they were unable to get any more height, and they decided that, whatever the map might say, they would have to find a way back through the maze of valleys and peaks.

They started to work their way up a valley. The moon threw shafts of light ahead and seemed at first to point the way, but soon the ground below seemed to gather itself together and fling itself up to make a barrier before them, a great mountain standing with its back to them, its broad shoulders shutting off all progress. They were forced to turn to port and follow the line of another valley, hoping it would lead them round the massive peak that had barred their way.

After a few minutes this valley, too, became more shallow, and soon the ground rolled up ahead of them like a wave. Again they turned, and again they found a promising valley, only to find that it came to a dead end. They were roaming up and down the valleys with continual changes of course, looking for means of escape and finding none, like a caged animal, all sense of direction gone. Much more of this and there wouldn't be enough petrol to get back home even if they could find a way through.

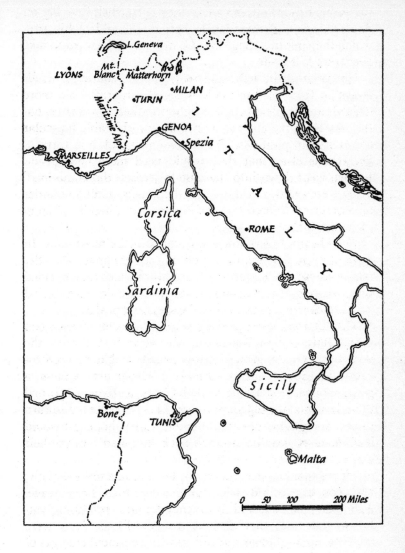

'We've got to get out of the mountains,' said Larden. 'The direction doesn't matter.' He and Mitchem scanned the undulating silhouette of the horizon for the lowest range in sight. It looked as though they might just clear the end of the valley in which they were flying, and they held their course.

'It's no use,' said Mitchem as the ground rose ahead of them, 'we can't get the height.' In desperation he increased the revs on the port outer, the only motor that was responding to the throttle levers, and they went into a crabbing, climbing turn to the right, while Mitchem held as straight a course as possible by a compensating pressure on the rudder bars.

The ground still rose above them as they climbed towards it. But it was too late to turn. Their only chance lay in the continuance of this staggering, drifting climb to the right.

They could see the moonlight glinting on the rocks beneath them, feel the sudden sensation of speed as the pass rose to meet them. Then the ground reared up under the nose as they flew on towards the pass in stalling attitude. Every moment they expected to feel the shattering crunch as the belly of the Stirling struck solid rock.

The two gunners watched the rocks slipping by beneath them faster and faster as the height separation decreased. They too were hardly able to sit in their seats, dreading the collision from below. But suddenly the men up front saw a huge open plain spread out before them, which proved to be a wide expanse of sea. They were through the pass and clear of the mountains at last.

But they had no idea where they were, or where to make for. They couldn't get back to England now. Larden went back to the navigator's table and discussed their position with Guy, and a further study of the coastline soon gave him his pinpoint. They were off La Spezia, on the North Italian coast. Somehow they must have come right through the Maritime Alps.

'We'd better make for Sicily,' said Larden. But when he

studied the maps and charts he found that they finished half way down the leg of Italy. Finding Sicily would be the purest guesswork, and in any case they had no idea which airfields were in Allied hands. He drew some lines on a chart to project the leg of Italy down into the Mediterranean, ending in the well-remembered heel and toe. Exactly where was Sicily? Surely it lay directly off to the toe? He drew in a blob to represent Sicily and took the result forward to agree a course with Mitchem. Then Guy suggested steering due south for a time while he tried to get a bearing, and they turned on to one-eight-zero. Guy had been given the frequency and call-sign of the radio station at Bone in North Africa for use in emergency.

Their situation remained desperate. They had no pilot and no navigator, no maps of the area into which they were flying and no idea of distances. Even if they succeeded in reaching an Allied airfield they still had to get the aircraft down. Their practice dual in flying the Stirling, now proving so invaluable, did not extend to experience of an approach and landing, and with Aaron completely incapacitated they would want to avoid baling out.

Clearly their biggest immediate concern was fuel. How long had they got in which to find a place to land? Had any of the petrol tanks been holed in the firing? As Larden took over in the first pilot's seat and headed out over the sea, Mitchem went back to check his fuel gauges. But when he saw, in the lights of the fuselage interior, the terrible injuries that Aaron had received, and the pain he was suffering, he decided that the first priority was an injection of morphia for his skipper. He took the ampoule and a hypodermic needle from the first-aid box and with Guy's help gave Aaron the injection. Only then did he turn to his engineer's panel.

So far as he could see there had been no damage, and although petrol consumption had been well above normal it had not been unduly excessive. Fortunately the engines had been set at cruise power at the time of the attack, and the two inboard motors, over which they had no control, were behaving normally. They had been airborne for nearly five hours and could hope for a maximum of perhaps another three hours airborne time. This, they thought, might be enough for them to find Sicily. As far as they were aware, everything else within striking distance was in enemy hands except Malta, which was notoriously difficult to find.

Much depended on what help they could get by radio. Guy had already sent a message to base telling them that the navigator was dead and the pilot badly wounded and that they were steering south, but he had received no answer, and he had had little success with Malta or Bone. Both stations were audible and appeared to be answering him, but he couldn't understand them, nor they him. They were using different codes.

He called Larden. 'Shall I try them in plain language?' It was against orders, but this was an emergency. 'Yes.'

As soon as Guy started to transmit in clear he got a reply from Bone. He told them that they were making for Sicily but that they had no maps. Was there some station in Sicily from which they could get a bearing? He was told to wait, and then after a minute or so came the reply. 'Advise against attempting to land Sicily. Too dangerous. Mountains and high ground, fighting still going on and airfield situation fluid. Advise you keep going for Bone in Eastern Algeria. Please transmit for bearing.'

When the first rough course to steer to reach Bone came through it was an unreliable third-class bearing, but it involved no more than a four-degree change of course – from 180 degrees to 184. Bone must be roughly due south of them, so they had guessed wrong about the position of Sicily, which must be south-east of them, to port. But the thought of crossing the Mediterranean dismayed them. North Africa seemed so far distant as to be unattainable.

'Ask them how far it is,' said Larden. But where from, since they didn't know their own position? He corrected himself. 'Ask them how far it is from La Spezia. We can work it out from there.'

Bone gave the distance from La Spezia as 500 miles, and Larden worked it out that they must now be about 400 miles from Bone. At their present rate of progress this meant at least another three hours in the air. Could they make it? Mitchem consulted his fuel gauges again and announced that they had little hope of getting there. But now they were in contact with Bone there was a good chance of being picked up if they came down in the sea.

In the meantime Aaron, although extremely weak from loss of blood and quite unable to talk, had recovered sufficiently to take an interest in their affairs. Because of the shattered windscreen the noise in the aircraft was deafening, and Guy wrote a note for him to say that they were making for North Africa. Aaron signalled for pencil and paper and began to scratch a few spidery letters with his left hand, which Guy was able to decipher. 'How can we navigate?' Guy showed him the makeshift map and the bearings from Bone, which were now coming through regularly. The effort of concentration exhausted Aaron and he lay back again and closed his eyes.

They kept going steadily, reducing height to 3000 feet to make the flight less distressing for Aaron. Mitchem drained all the smaller fuel tanks into the four main tanks and turned all the cross-feeds on, so that the engines would run to the last drop of petrol, and now they were clear of danger from fighters McCabe came forward to watch the warning lights on the fuel indicators, while Richmond took a turn at flying the aircraft. The moon had gone now and it was pitch dark, so that they couldn't see the water, and for much of the time they were in fact crossing straight over Corsica and Sardinia, though they saw nothing.

About an hour later they were aware of an inverted pyramid of light deep in the horizon, at a vast distance, floodlighting the sky. This they took to be the searchlight system at Bone, acting as a beacon to guide them in. But as the shaft of night came nearer, it seemed that they had made the crossing of the Mediterranean remarkably quickly. Either they had a strong following wind or the searchlights were on Sardinia.

To make absolutely sure, they flew straight on past the searchlights when they reached them, while Guy asked for further bearings. Straight away he got a reciprocal and they knew that they must indeed have reached Bone. The hazards of the sea crossing were behind them.

But now came the most dangerous moments of all. Larden called the rest of the crew on the inter-com. 'Well, fellers, what are we going to do? Are we going to bale out or what?'

'We can't leave the skipper.'

'Couldn't we drop him by static line?'

'We'd never get him out.'

'It's hopeless to bale out.'

'What do you say, then?' asked Larden. 'Shall I try and do a belly-landing?'

'That's the best thing.'

'OK by me.'

'Me too. Either we all get down or we all go for the chop.'

They were still unaware that in the bomb-racks lay the unseen menace of the 4000-pound secret bomb, which in the course of a belly-landing might well go off.

Meanwhile Larden and Mitchem were describing figures of eight over Bone so as not to lose sight of the airfield and losing height simultaneously. The searchlights had been switched off but the runway was marked by two parallel lines of flares. It was mutually agreed that it should be Larden who attempted the actual touchdown, aided as far as possible by Mitchem. Both men feared the difficulties and dangers of the approach as much as the landing. They called airfield control repeatedly and asked for instructions but could get no reply.

Although they had originally decided on a wheels-up landing, familiarity with the controls had increased their confidence and they begun to consider whether they might not attempt to use the undercarriage. This would be a neater but much more critical operation. If successful it would avoid any further damage to Stirling 'O for Oboe'. But if it failed the resultant crash might be far more serious and would be much more likely to cause fatalities. Nevertheless they might well have taken the risk had they known about the unreleased bomb. But first they had trouble in letting down the undercarriage, which had evidently been damaged in the firing, and then Guy got a message through from the ground station giving landing instructions. 'There's a crashed Wellington blocking the end of the runway,' he told Larden. 'The safe runway length is reduced to 700 yards.'

'That settles it,' said Larden. 'It's a wheels-up landing.'

As the left-hand windscreen was shattered, Larden decided to attempt the landing from the right-hand seat. He changed placed with Mitchem. 'I shan't land on the strip,' he said, 'I shall put her down to the left of the runway. Then I can look across to the right and use the runway lights as a guide.' That way he would have the lights in view right up to the touch-down.

But while they were circling to lose height prior to the final approach, Aaron, conscious of the clumsy manoeuvring and the change of altitude, signalled to Guy to ask what was happening. Guy wrote out a message for him. 'Everything all right, we're over land and we'll be down in a minute.'

Still unable to speak, Aaron struggled to raise himself from the floor. He could scarcely move, but he motioned to Guy, and it was clear that he felt his place was up front. He was pointing forward with his left hand and trying to crawl, and indicating to Guy that he wished to be helped into the pilot's seat.

Guy called Larden. 'The skipper's worried. He wants to come up front. What shall I do?'

'If he can get up here, let him. He might be able to help with the approach. He might even be able to do the landing.'

Mitchem got out of the left-hand seat and went back to help Guy and the two gunners lift Aaron forward. Larden stayed in the right-hand seat. Aaron would thus be exposed to the slipstream, but it was obvious that he must sit in his customary seat.

Helped by his entire crew, Aaron struggled back into the cockpit. His face, practically shot in two, was black with caked blood, his right forearm was held on by no more than a few pieces of tendon. Yet none of the crew would deny him the right to take charge of the approach and landing. Indeed they welcomed it. Whether he was able to carry it through or not, his presence in the left-hand seat was of immense psychological value to them all.

Applying the necessary pressure to the control column with his left hand, Aaron began the let-down. He could not speak, he had no free hand to gesticulate, and the only way in which he could communicate with Larden was by movements of the head. Thus he made his approach, flying out of the darkness down towards the narrow plank of runway indicated by the parallel lights, while the rest of the crew took up their crash positions in the fuselage on orders from Larden.

They had worked out a drill for the vital seconds immediately after the landing. As soon as the aircraft came to a standstill, McCabe, Richmond and Guy would escape through the roof hatch in the rear and then crawl along the top of the fuselage to the front roof hatch, where Larden and Mitchem would be lifting Aaron out. The three men on top of the fuselage would pull Aaron clear and then Larden and Mitchem would follow. If they had time before any possible fire they would lift Brennan out as well.

The crippled Stirling floated gently down towards the runway lights, coaxed by the dying Aaron – for dying he must surely be. Larden could not imagine how anyone could take such punishment and still retain his senses. And indeed he was beginning to realise that Aaron could not possibly have done so, and that he was flying simply by instinct and an indomitable sense of duty. Larden could not get it across to him that they had no undercarriage and very little throttle control, and Aaron was clearly intending to land on the runway.

Dissatisfied with his approach, and perhaps distracted by Larden's efforts to get him to land off the runway, Aaron began to ease back the stick and nod towards the throttles with the evident intention of going round again. Obediently Larden pushed the throttles forward, but the only engine answering properly to the controls was still the port outer, and the effect of a sudden burst of power in this one engine was to skid the aircraft sideways to starboard across the runway. The lights disappeared beneath them and they flew on into utter darkness.

Fortunately Aaron had made a powered approach well above stalling speed and the increased power put them into a gentle climb. Larden watched while Aaron, apparently as cool and determined as ever, began the protracted business of getting the Stirling lined up for another approach, at the right speed, distance, and height, and with practically no throttle control. Only now did Larden realise how impossible this approach would have been for him and Mitchem.

Somehow Aaron managed to bank the Stirling round in a right-handed horseshoe, while Larden watched the instruments uneasily, and at length they were again lined up on the runway.

Before they settled down on the final approach Larden went through an elaborate pantomime to indicate to Aaron that the undercarriage was jammed and that the far end of the runway was blocked, and that it might be better to land off the runway, but Aaron's injuries and the effects of the morphia had robbed him of any understanding other than the instinct of duty. There was also the danger, becoming more acute with every moment, that they would run out of petrol, and Larden tried to explain this, but could not tell if it was comprehended. Then at the last moment, for the second time, with all the crew at crash stations, Aaron eased back the stick and nodded towards the throttles to indicate that he was going round again. Larden pushed the throttles forward and they swayed drunkenly across the runway and out into the darkness.

Mitchem's anxiety about their fuel situation had grown to the certainty that the next approach would be their last. He was getting continual blinks on the petrol warning lights and none of the gauges were registering at all. In a moment the engines would cut and then they would have to land straight ahead – supposing that Aaron and Larden were able to retain any control at all. He had heard the last-minute changes of engine note and had wondered what was going on, and now he went forward and shouted above the slipstream at Aaron and Larden.

'The tanks are bone dry. If you don't land on the next approach I'm ordering the rest of the crew to bale out.'

Aaron completed yet another circuit and approach and the Stirling purred downwards towards the runway lights, the warm desert air pouring in through the windscreen. This time Mitchem stood behind Aaron, pressed up as close as possible behind his seat to counteract the expected deceleration, gripping Aaron round the chest in case he was thrown forward, and keeping his right arm free to prevent Aaron from attempting to go round again once they were down near the runway. But even so, twenty or thirty feet from the ground, when Mitchem had withdrawn his hand to brace himself for the crash, Aaron began to pull back on the control column with the pilot's instinctive reaction to a landing which he felt was fundamentally unsafe.

'There's no petrol for another circuit,' screamed Larden, 'go down. Go down !' Aaron shook his head and continued to pull back, nodding towards the throttles for the third time. In utter desperation Larden leaned across and thumped Aaron back from the control column. Aaron collapsed completely, but not before he had turned a look on Larden that the Canadian would never forget.

By the time Larden had gained control the aircraft was fifty feet up and on the point of stalling. Again they had crabbed to starboard across the runway. The port wing was dropping and Larden pushed the controls hard forward. They were well to the right of the runway, in the extreme darkness beyond the lights.

'We can't be far out,' shouted Larden, 'I'll put her down here.'

He held on as they gained speed, driving down into the blackness, and then when he judged that the ground was near, he pulled back. There was a grinding, scraping noise underneath, like a ship running aground, followed by two solid bumps, and then their forward momentum had been arrested and they were choking in a dense cloud of dust.

The unreleased bomb had not gone off.

The three men in the back of the plane were out of the rear roof hatch in seconds and scrambling forward along the top of the fuselage, feeling their way in the darkness, the clouds of suspended dust gritting in their mouths and smarting in their eyes. Larden and Mitchem, with Aaron's dead weight to support, were longer in getting to their hatch, but soon the three men outside were reaching down and lifting Aaron by his parachute straps until they could rest him on top of the fuselage. The belly-landing meant that they were near the ground and when Larden and Mitchem were out of the hatch they lifted Aaron off his perch and passed him down to the three men waiting below. Then they too jumped clear. There was no sign of fire.

It was Richmond who broke the tension. 'Eee,' he said, his Yorkshire accent more pronounced than ever, 'we've had worse rides on a double-decker bus.' Elated at their escape, they had time to laugh before remembering that the body of their dead navigator was still inside the aircraft. They went back and carried Brennan out.

The first light was seeping in over the horizon as the ambulances arrived. They took Aaron away quickly in the first ambulance, but there was nothing they could do for him, and nine hours later he died. Terrible as his external injuries were, it was the chest wounds that killed him. Had he been content to give in, had he abandoned the attempt to do his duty as he saw it and lain still in the fuselage, instead of taking charge of the perilous final approach, medical opinion was that he might have lived. But it wasn't in him to do so. Nor could his crew restrain him.

The responsibility for the destruction done to Stirling 'O for Oboe' and its crew was never pinned down with any certainty, possibly because the gunner on whom suspicion fell went missing before an enquiry could be held. How often this sort of tragedy occurred is unknown, but it is probable that, like mid-air collision, it was yet another of the countless hazards that all bomber crews had to face. A gunner who caught himself dozing, or who was suffering from oxygen lack, could well be guilty of a tragic mistake.

The incident had occurred on an operational flight, over the target, and there was the remote possibility that it had not been accidental – that it could in fact be attributed to some sort of enemy action. Rumours that the enemy had infiltrated captured British bombers into our bomber stream for just this purpose had been heard. So when it came to recognition of the courage displayed by Aaron and his crew, the incident was treated as due to enemy action, and most of the crew were decorated. Allan Larden got the Conspicuous Gallantry Medal, and the DFM went to Mitchem and Guy.

There was only one medal that could go to Arthur Aaron, and no one who knew the story can possibly have doubted that it was the right one. On 14 December 1943 he was posthumously awarded the Victoria Cross.

# 9

## *Bill Reid*

FOR FOUR HOURS the afternoon sun, little more than an aperture in the heavens now that November had come, had shed on the bare Nottinghamshire landscape much of the warmth of late summer. The crews of No. 61 Squadron at Syerston had walked down to briefing without overcoats or Irving jackets, sweating a little beneath their white roll-top jerseys. But now, as they hurried from the messes down to the flight offices, the taste of bacon and eggs and hot tea still in their throats, they felt the chill clamminess of winter. A pall of mist that did not seem to threaten fog hung around the airfield and the washy cobalt of the sky had deepened with the approach of night.

They had been briefed for a raid on Düsseldorf. Following the loss of 125 aircraft in three raids on Berlin, Harris had turned for the moment to targets nearer home. Tonight, 3 November 1943, would be yet another mutation in the eternal compromise which constituted the bomber offensive.

Some revision of the policy for the area bombing of big industrial targets, laid down in February 1942, had been forced on Harris by heavy losses due to the increasing size and efficiency of the German night-fighter force, itself a product of the bomber offensive. The Me 110 and the Ju 88 had been made available in large numbers. The FW 190, armed with four 20-millimetre cannon, had begun to roam the German night skies. And the early haphazard nature of German air interception had gone, replaced by accurate airborne radar devices and astute ground control. Opportunist free-lance fighters, tipped off by radio from a reorganised ground observer corps, harried the bomber routes.

Batteries of searchlights illuminated the bomber streams and the once frustrated fighters carried flares to help them sight their prey. In any one night over Germany some 500 skilled night-fighter pilots lay in wait for the bombers, their lethal technique of attacking from below, out of the darkness, now perfected. The Americans were suffering even more disastrously by day, and it became clear that unless German aircraft production could be checked the whole bomber offensive would founder. Hence from mid-June 1943 the main weight of Bomber Command's attack was switched whenever possible to industrial areas contributing directly to German aircraft production.

Five months later, however, the effects of this policy had proved disappointing. The results of the British area attacks at night and the American pinpoint bombing by day could only be long-term in any case, and even these had been restricted by frequent diversions of effort. The German day and night fighter forces remained strong and active and the Americans, appalled by their heavy losses in October, began to seek closer co-ordination between the day and night offensives and a general revision of the plan. Quite apart from the bomber offensive as such, the destruction of the German fighter force remained imperative if the invasion of France was to take place in six months' time.

It was with the knowledge that the German fighters presented a more deadly threat than ever before that nearly 600 bombers approached the Dutch coast on the night of 3 November 1943 on their way to Düsseldorf.

The mathematical logic which proclaimed that few if any crews could hope to complete a tour of thirty operations left most men undismayed. That kind of arithmetic only worked for the other fellow. The average crew-man looked no further than the successful completion of the night's raid.

So it was with Flight Lieutenant Bill Reid, a tall, relaxed Scot from Baillieston, Glasgow, whose apparent maturity belied his twenty-one years. No one would have guessed, either, that he had only recently converted on to Lancasters and that this was no more than his tenth operational sortie. Already he had about him the phlegmatic assurance of the veteran.

Twenty-one-thousand feet beneath them the crew glimpsed through patches of cloud the crazy paving of the Dutch islands south of Rotterdam, large slabs of land separated by thin channels of water. They had crossed the enemy coast. By way of greeting, two orange flares floated gently down from above them like planets cut adrift, lighting up the sky by day. Obviously there was a German fighter up there, waiting like an eagle to swoop on its prey. Emerson, in the rear turret, and Baldwin, in the mid-upper, intensified their search for aircraft, while Reid banked to port and starboard to help the two gunners cover the blind spots underneath.

'There's a fighter dead astern.' It was Emerson from the rear turret. There was a fault in his turret heating, and in those fatal seconds his fingers were too cold to operate the trigger mechanism. He managed to swing the turret into line, but it was too late. In the same instant there was a blinding flash in the cockpit and an unseen fist struck Reid a sledge-hammer blow in the shoulder and he crumpled forward over the control column. Simultaneously Emerson and Baldwin opened fire from point-blank range as the fighter broke away to starboard.

'Hell.' The single epithet escaped Reid's lips and was transmitted to the crew over the inter-com as the Lancaster lunged downward under the pressure of Reid's weight on the stick. His head felt queer and incomplete, as though the top of his skull had been blown off, the wind was lashing through the broken windscreen, fragments of Perspex were embedded in his face and hands. He struggled to get his goggles on to protect his eyes. Blood was pouring down his face and leaking into his oxygen mask and the taste of it was salt and bitter in his mouth. Half-choked and gasping for breath, he tore the mask away.

'Are you all right, Bill?'

Alan Jeffries, the navigator, a schoolteacher from Western Australia, was calling him. He braced himself in his seat and pulled the Lancaster out of the dive. They had lost 2000 feet.

'Yes, I feel all right. Is everybody OK?'

One by one the crew-members answered that they were unhurt. 'It was an Me 110,' said Emerson. 'He was right on top of us.' Emerson had already completed a bombing tour and was the most experienced man in the crew. 'My fingers were frozen – I couldn't pull the trigger until he was almost gone. But I'm certain I hit him.'

'So am I,' called Baldwin.

Reid said nothing about his own injuries. There was no point. He had already decided to go on. The aircraft seemed all right and he didn't feel too bad – just a bit light-headed, that was all. The intense cold had staunched the flow of blood from his head and congealed the rivulets on his face. If he turned back he would only be a danger to the rest of the bomber stream.

He called Jeffries. 'Check on that course again will you, Jeff?'

'Roger.'

Jeffries, a teetotaller and non-smoker, was the fittest man in the crew. Yet every time he flew he was airsick. It made no difference to his work, nor to his determination to finish his tour. A married man, he wrote daily to his wife back in Perth. He was a fine cricketer, and his ambition to play one day at Lord's had been fulfilled that summer when he had represented the Royal Australian Air Force. Another member of the team had been Keith Miller.

They went on steering slightly south of east for Düsseldorf. But German fighters were still harrying the stream.

'F.W. 190 on port beam.' The call came from Baldwin and Emerson together, but they had only got their glimpse at the last minute. Both turrets had been damaged in the first attack and accurate aiming was impossible, but each man had a serviceable gun and each got in a single burst.

The Lancaster had been hit again. The FW 190 had caught them broadside, showering the fuselage with cannon from stem to stern. Reid, struck all over the body with shell fragments, lost control of the crippled Lancaster and once again it plunged earthwards.

Norris, the Welsh flight engineer, although badly wounded in the arm, grabbed one side of the control column and tried to help Reid recover control. Rolton, the baby-faced bomb-aimer, at nineteen still little more than a boy, was thrown forward in the nose and looked up to see Norris and Reid struggling with the stick. Forgetting his own wounds, he hurried back to help. One of the elevators had been shot away and the aircraft's natural flying attitude had developed into a steep dive. The Lancaster had also developed a pronounced yaw to starboard and instinctively Reid applied hard left rudder to correct it. Three times the falling Lancaster circled in a flat spin while Norris and Rolton and the half-conscious Reid tried to recover control. They hauled back on the control column with all their strength, but they couldn't keep their grip on it and finally Reid jammed it between his knees. He turned to Norris and Rolton, gave them the thumbs-up sign, and then fainted. He had been without oxygen for several minutes.

While this drama was being fought out in the cockpit, Baldwin was extricating himself from the damaged mid-upper turret and picking his way forward to see what had happened in the front compartment. In the dim interior lighting he could see two apparently lifeless figures slumped on top of each other like sacks of coal on the fuselage floor. Underneath was Jeffries, the navigator. Sprawled across him was Mann, the wireless operator.

It was clear that Jeffries would never play cricket again. Mann was still breathing but looked in bad shape. Only three weeks before they had gone up to his home in Liverpool to celebrate his twenty-first birthday.

Baldwin pulled Mann back into his seat, stuck an oxygen tube in his mouth, and clipped on his parachute. The whole of his wireless equipment had been blown out. Then Baldwin knelt down to confirm what he already knew – that Jeffries was dead.

Going forward to report to Reid, Baldwin found Norris and Rolton still struggling to keep control. He shouted into Norris's ear. 'Can you cope?'

'I think so.'

'I'm going back to help Emerson.'

Baldwin made his way back through the fuselage, staring in astonishment at the moon, which was shining through the holes in the fuselage torn by the fighter's 20-millimetre cannon. He rapped on the turret door, and when there was no answer he rapped again. At last the doors opened and there was Emerson, smiling and giving the thumbs up. Baldwin went back to his turret, operating it manually to keep a look out for aircraft, and to keep warm.

Twice Reid recovered consciousness but each time he fainted again. Norris grabbed a portable oxygen container and fitted it to the tube of Reid's oxygen mask. Eventually Reid recovered sufficiently to fly the aircraft with Norris's help. Rolton went back into the nose.

Reid had to keep the control column right back in his stomach to hold the aircraft straight and level. It still did not occur to him to turn back.

His navigator was dead and his wireless operator seriously, perhaps fatally, injured, but he was not properly aware of this. All he knew was that they were hurt and that he could expect no help from them. He and his flight engineer were both severely injured. The aircraft was badly damaged and barely controllable. Both the compasses had packed up. The inter-com had been severed and he had no contact with his gunners. But by reference to the Pole Star he brought the Lancaster round on to roughly the correct course and steered again for Düsseldorf.

Baldwin and Emerson stayed in their turrets. They could not communicate with Reid but each still had a serviceable gun. The Lancaster was now flying just above a broken layer of cloud which at least gave them some protection from below.

Reid began to look for a pinpoint to lead them in to the target. He remembered that at briefing they had been told that spoof flares were being dropped on Cologne to draw off the fighters, so he checked again with the Pole Star and then steered for Cologne. Soon he recognised the bend of the river and picked out the bridges through a break in the cloud. The spoof flares were still going down over Cologne so he couldn't be so very far out in his timing. He turned to port on to 060 degrees to head for Düsseldorf, and within a minute or so began to pick out the black outline of other Lancasters. He was back in the bomber stream.

He pulled the handle to open the bomb-doors and signalled to Norris, who reached down with his foot to touch Rolton and attract his attention. When Rolton looked up, Reid pointed ahead at the target and signalled to him to get ready for the bombing run. The cloud had disappeared and visibility was good except for ground haze. To the right they could see the Rhine again, working out its course northwards. Directly ahead was the target. Red and green target indicators were still going down.

With Norris's help Reid held the Lancaster straight and level and they flew slap over the centre of the target. The opposition seemed to be unco-ordinated and the flak isolated, though the sky was criss-crossed like a skating rink with the blades of searchlights. The fighters seemed to have spent themselves along the route. Perhaps those spoof flares over Cologne had worked.

Reid felt the cockpit lift slightly as the bombs fell off, but he still held the aircraft steady. Down in the nose the willing Rolton, fresh-faced as a choirboy, was taking his picture of the attack.

After a full minute Reid turned for home, steering a more northerly course to avoid the worst of the defences, guided again by the Pole Star. But he was extremely weak now from loss of blood, and the emergency supply of oxygen had run out, so that the effort of holding both arms round the control column with his hands clasped to give greater purchase proved too much for him. Several times he passed out. Each time Norris held on as best he could, often with Rolton's help, until Reid recovered.

Crossing the Dutch coast they were buffeted by the blast from heavy flak but they escaped being hit. They were descending all the time, and as soon as they were clear of the enemy coast Reid put the nose down still farther to get below oxygen height. They were half-way across the Channel when all four engines suddenly cut dead.

All the fight had gone from Reid and he relaxed in his seat, content that the struggle should end. Loss of blood and lack of oxygen had left him light-headed and the vague thought of crashing into the North Sea left him unmoved. It was Norris, the flight engineer, who realised what had happened and moved quickly to correct it. He had forgotten to switch the petrol cocks over. He, too had been affected by lack of oxygen. The Lancaster had absolutely no vices and as soon as the petrol supply came through again the engines picked up and the aircraft flew on.

As they descended and the oxygen content increased Reid began to think about the landing. The hydraulics had gone and that meant pumping the undercarriage down, also the flaps. The brakes would be useless. The bomb-doors were open, making the aircraft even more difficult to control. He would need a long runway.

The biggest runway he knew of was Wittering. He tried to write the word 'Wittering' with his finger on the broken windscreen but he could not make the crew understand. Rolton and Norris stood beside him, watching for the first sign of the coast. Suddenly they saw a flashing light, and then away to the right a cone of searchlights, indicating an airfield. Norris pointed to the petrol gauges, which were showing empty. Reid turned north to head towards the searchlights. There was no time to look for Wittering. They had better try to get down.

Beyond the fact that they were somewhere over the East Coast they had little idea where they were. They were down to about 4000 feet now, and as they circled the searchlights they saw the runway lights and sodium flares leading them in. Reid pulled the air bottle and pumped the undercarriage down; then he pumped down 20 degrees of flap. The exertion, coupled with the fact they they were now below freezing level, started his head bleeding again. He flashed his landing light as a distress signal, pointed downwards to the crew, and began a long approach, keeping the engine revolutions up and gliding flatly down. The open bomb-doors were causing additional drag and giving a ballooning effect to the approach, but he was well lined up on the runway. Norris and Rolton braced themselves immediately behind him, ready to grab the controls if he should faint. Emerson, the old hand, came out of his turret to take up his crash position. Seeing that Baldwin was still in his turret he walked forward and shouted to him to come out. The two men braced themselves amidships.

As Reid touched down the undercarriage collapsed. It had been shot through in the fighter attack. The Lancaster slid along the runway for fifty to sixty yards and then came to rest.

They had landed at an American airfield in Norfolk. They climbed out of the top hatch, and not till then did Reid know that Jeffries was dead. The wounded men were rushed to hospital. Reid was given a blood transfusion, his shoulder was cleaned up and his head wounds stitched. Mann, the wireless operator, died next day.

Reid's first visitor was his group commander, Air Vice-Marshal the Hon. Ralph Cochrane. Cochrane brought the news that the photographs taken by Rolton showed that their bombs had fallen fair and square on the target.

'Why didn't you turn back?' asked Cochrane. Reid had to admit that he had scarcely thought of it.

Cochrane plied Reid with questions and got the full story of the flight. He was so impressed with the actions of the whole crew that he recommended a number of awards, but the first Reid knew of it was six weeks later when, still in hospital, he was visited by a public relations man. 'Normally I send my flying officer when it's a DFC,' said the PR man, 'and when it's a DSO I send my flight lieutenant.' He indicated his badges of rank. 'See what I've got here?' Reid looked down at the two and a half rings of a squadron leader. But the significance was lost on him, and he was astonished when a day or so later he heard he had been awarded the VC.

\* \* \*

When Reid recovered he was sent on a month's leave. Towards the end of the fourth week he was asked to take the salute at a march-past of ATC cadets and Cadet Corps boys in Hampden Park, Glasgow. This meant over-staying his leave, and he cabled group headquarters to ask for an extension. The reply was uncompromising. 'Return to unit immediately. Call group headquarters on the way.'

At Moreton Hall he was thrust before the group commander. 'How are you?' asked Cochrane. 'Fully recovered? Feeling fit again?'

'Yes, fine, thank you.'

'You must be fed up with all this publicity.'

'I am, rather.'

'Well, I've got a job for you. I want you for 617.'

So Cochrane hadn't got him his VC for nothing! The shrewd Reid appreciated the way Cochrane's mind had worked. He knew that the dam-busting squadron was Cochrane's special pride and care. And underneath that casual Scots exterior he was thrilled at the compliment.

'Fine.'

'Is there anyone you'd particularly like to take with you?'

'Yes – my bomb-aimer, Les Rolton. He's been with me since OTU, and he's keen to stay with me. He's the best crew man I know.'

So the keen, boyish Rolton with the ready smile joined

Reid at 617. The other survivors of his crew had scattered. Norris was grounded because of his injuries. Emerson and Baldwin had gone back to the squadron to complete their tour. Emerson was already missing.

Another man Reid asked for was a wireless operator named David Luker whom he had met at his operational training unit. He wrote to Luker, who jumped at the chance.

On 617 they operated only occasionally, mostly in support of the invasion, and during the next four months only two crews were lost. Then on 31 July 1944 they were briefed to attack a flying bomb storage dump in a railway tunnel at Rilly La Montagne, near Rheims. 9 Squadron were to bomb the northern end of the tunnel and 617 the southern, the object being to seal the tunnel. Both squadrons were to drop 12,000-pound 'Tallboys'. The main force were to drop delayed-action bombs which would hamper the work of clearing the blocked tunnel and which might set off the V-weapons. Willie Tait and Bill Duffy were to do the marking, but when they got there they found the visibility so good and the tunnel entrances so clearly delineated that any atttempt at marking could only confuse a clear issue. They took their markers home.

The main force were stepped up to 18,000 feet. Reid had been briefed to go in at 12,000. To drop the 'Tallboy' accurately meant a straight and level run of four and a half minutes, and the crew settled down to it resignedly, ignoring the black puffs of flak that sailed by like islands in the sky. They had been told at briefing that they need not bother with pictures, but this wasn't good enough for Rolton, who, as at Düsseldorf, liked to see his bombing results confirmed.

'Hold it !'

Rolton was still stretched out on his stomach in the nose. Reid was still holding the Lancaster steady. Everyone in the aircraft was counting the seconds, impatient for the moment when Reid could start taking evasive action and turn away from the target. But the inter-com was still silent as Rolton waited for his picture when suddenly the whole aircraft rocked and shook as though it had been hit by a bomb. The simile occurred to Reid, and in the same instant he realised its aptness. This was exactly what had happened.

A thousand-pounder dropped by an aircraft of the main force six thousand feet above them had crashed through the top of the fuselage between the cockpit and the mid-upper turret and careered on through the floor. The structure of the aircraft round its centre of gravity had been fatally weakened and the control wires had been severed, leaving Reid with a floppy, wobbling stick and an aircraft wallowing and uncontrollable.

'Stand by to bale out!'

'Chunky' Stewart, the flight engineer, handed him his parachute in a swift, disciplined movement. Reid pushed and pulled again on the control column and turned it fully left and right, but there was not the smallest answer from the control surfaces. There was no point in delaying the jump. With the fuselage holed from top to bottom the aircraft might break up at any moment.

'Bale out! Bale out!'

Peltier, the French Canadian navigator, appeared from the wrecked fuselage and hurried down towards the hatch in the nose, Stewart followed. Luker, the wireless operator, came forward and stood next to Reid, waiting for Stewart to get down into the nose before following him. With the redistribution of weight of the crew, the Lancaster gently nose-dived, spiralling downwards.

It was too late to alter the weight distribution. As the dive steepened, the downward pressure threw Reid forward, preventing him from moving across the cockpit to the passage down into the nose. He was trapped in his seat.

He thought of the dinghy escape hatch, in the roof just behind him. Probably it had been buckled and jammed by the bomb. He struggled out of his seat, reached upwards, grabbed the handle, and turned it clockwise.

The speed of the Lancaster had built up dangerously in the dive. The suction when Reid opened the roof hatch was terrific. He felt its cyclonic force tear him from his seat and drag him rapidly upwards. There was a sibilant, whirring sound in his ears, then everything was incredibly peaceful and he was falling freely through space.

He groped for the cord-handle of his 'chute and pulled. Nothing happened. He felt like a man who had turned a door handle only to find it fall loose in his hand. Then suddenly there was an explosion above him, then a jerk and a fluttering of sails. He was floating on air.

Bits of the Lancaster were crashing down past him towards the ground. The aircraft must have broken up as he opened the hatch. He couldn't see any other parachutes but the others must have got out before him.

He had struck his right hand on the hatch when he was sucked out of the plane, numbing it so that he could not control his descent. He landed in the top of a tree. He slid carefully down the trunk and fell safely in soft earth. As he got up he could hear the bombs still going off on the target. He took off his parachute and Mae West and hid them under a bush. The bombing run had been from west to east so he must be some miles east of the target. He looked for a way south through the trees.

He unpeeled the shell dressing in his battle-dress pocket and bandaged his hand. Then he pulled out his escape kit and studied the compass. He had gone about a mile and was just emerging into a clearing when he was suddenly faced not twenty yards away by three Germans, standing there belligerently, rifles and bayonets at the ready. His escape bid was over.

The Germans took him to a nearby flak station. As they walked along the edge of the wood, Reid saw the tail of a Lancaster sticking out of the trees. He asked to see it, and the Germans took him over. It was part of his own aircraft. The rear turret was about sixty yards from the main tail section, and Reid stared at it in horrified disbelief. The gunner was still in it.

He tramped over to the main tail section. The mid-upper

gunner lay in the fuselage, slumped against the rear door. That was two of them who hadn't got out.

Half an hour later, at the flak station, the Germans brought in another prisoner. It was David Luker, the wireless operator. Like Reid he had been sucked out of the roof hatch when the aircraft broke up. There was no sign of the three men who had escaped from the front.

It was not until after the war that Reid learned that Peltier and Stewart, together with his old friend Les Folton, had perished in the nose of the Lancaster, unable to get out as it plunged earthwards.

# 10

## *Target Amiens*

F OR TWO DAYS the smooth drab surfaces of East Anglia and northern France had achieved even greater anonymity under heavy falls of snow. The whole muted countryside was one of vast steppe, broken only by the sprawling slate of the larger settlements and the black puddles of the towns. The sky was a slushy off-white, bloated with snow, shutting out the rays of the sun, leaving the whitewashed earth to throw off its own bright phosphorescence, day and night. From Brittany to Picardy the fields lay polished and still, unmarked as yet by the battles so soon to come. For once the crowded air of East Anglia was quiet and empty, like the streets of a city on Sunday, the warplanes grounded by blinding blizzards, their bases silent and immobilised in the grip of winter.

Yet individuality was still proclaimed by the occasional landmark. From London the military lorries clanked their heavy chains along the old Great North Road through Hertfordshire, contiguous with the petrified Mosquito airfield at Hunsden, near Ware. At Amiens the cathedral rose in unmistakable defiance, while spiky telegraph poles led north-eastwards, past the rectangular wall of the prison, along the deserted *Route d'Albert*.

Inside the prison languished some 700 French men and women, of whom about 250 were political prisoners, liable to a variety of sentences from deportation to execution by the firing squad. Often the latter was the more merciful. The number of prisoners under sentence of death was known only to the Germans. Estimates varied. It was known that eleven members of the *Francs Tireurs et Partisans Français* had

167

been shot in the jail in December 1943. It was also known that another batch of executions was imminent. It might be twenty, it might be fifty, it might be a hundred. But this was only half the story. For every man due to be shot, two or three others were awaiting a travesty of a trial before hearing the inevitable sentence. Deportation or death.

In the last weeks of 1943 the Resistance forces in the province of Somme had suffered crippling blows. One by one, with chilling efficiency, key men of the various groups in the province had been arrested by the Gestapo. Soon it was plain that there was an informer amongst them. The province had been one of the strongest Maquis areas in the whole of France. Now the morale of the various groups was severely shaken.

It was natural that the people of Picardy should have little love for the Germans. Their sufferings had been intense, first through invasion, then through occupation. Requisitioning had been especially severe in this area. The flat plains had been utilised for military preparations for the invasion of England that never came. Large tracts of agricultural land had been commandeered for the building of airfields for the bombing of London. Later, when the invasion was abandoned, the exercise areas were used for the training of divisions bound for the Eastern front.

Against this background of hardship and humiliation, Resistance groups mushroomed and prospered. All kinds of invaluable military information was passed to London by clandestine means. Prisoners-of-war escape routes were operated. Daring acts of sabotage against German military establishments and communications were mounted. Hundreds of German soldiers were killed in train crashes alone. But each success brought redoubled Gestapo efforts to track down the culprits, and at last they found their informer.

Dominique Ponchardier, leader of the whole of Occupied France of a group called the 'Sosies', in direct touch with British intelligence sources and undertaking sabotage and escape activities as well as espionage, realised that the Gestapo had struck a major blow at the forces of the Resistance, crippling so far as Somme province was concerned. Dark-haired and dark-skinned, with a pointed nose and chin that in determined moods almost seemed to meet, he began to consider a combined Maquis operation in which the walls of Amiens jail would be broken open, the guards overpowered and the prisoners released.

It would be an immense undertaking. Quite possibly it would fail. But without it, organised resistance in the province of Somme, and perhaps in the whole of northern France, would cease.

Ponchardier had hardly made his resolve when, in January 1944, in the adjacent province of Aisne, a similar operation was attempted by local Resistance forces against a jail at St Quentin. It was a disastrous failure. At once the guards at all the prisons throughout Occupied France were strengthened, and many more arrests were made. Nothing would persuade the average Resistance man to talk, but the Germans had their methods, and there were bound to be exceptions. Each captured Resistance man was a potential source of danger to those still free.

Ponchardier, and other men like him, although accustomed to the daily fear of discovery, now hardly dared to show themselves. Long-term planning became impossible, and the tragedy at St Quentin ruled out any such operation at Amiens. But Ponchardier, as befitted the ideal Resistance leader, was a man of cunning and resource. He soon decided that there was only one way of breaking into Amiens jail, and that was with bombs – the bombs of the RAF. Some time previously a direct request for a bombing operation in similar circumstances had been turned down as too dangerous for the prisoners. It was necessary to be oblique.

Ponchardier began sending through to London various details of the construction, lay-out and defences of Amiens jail, under the guise of routine reports. This was the kind of information he had sent through on scores of other targets, military and semi-military, and it aroused no comment. But the effect was that most of the information necessary for mounting a bombing operation against the jail was ready to hand in England. If, as a last resort, such an operation proved to be necessary, it could be planned in detail at short notice.

Early in February it became clear that nothing but an earthquake could save the condemned men in Amiens jail. It was known that the date for the next batch of executions had been fixed for 19 or 20 February. Ponchardier and the other Resistance leaders still at large pondered the situation, and Ponchardier put forward his scheme. An instinctive horror at the dangers inherent in such an attack, which must result in many deaths, perhaps amongst the innocent, or amongst those not in danger of their lives, was slowly overcome as the day fixed for the executions drew nearer and the complete absence of any practicable alternative became manifest. Added to this was the moral compulsion, felt by every Resistance man still at liberty, to try any scheme, however desperate, which might bring help to his comrades.

So early in February Ponchardier made his request to London. And he couched it in astute terms. He did not plead particularly for the men at Amiens. He stressed the frightful reverses suffered by the entire Resistances forces in recent weeks and the urgent need for some striking demonstration of the ability and willingness of the Allies to intervene. Amiens would be the *cause célèbre*. It was quite by chance that details of the target had already been transmitted to London.

In London the proposal met with scepticism and doubt. No one liked it. The Intelligence Service passed it to the Air Ministry. The Air Ministry passed it to Air Chief Marshal Sir Trafford Leigh-Mallory, commanding the Allied Expeditionary Air Force. Mallory passed it on to Air Marshal 'Mary' Coningham, commanding Second Tactical Air Force. Coningham passed it to Air Vice-Marshal Basil

Embry, AOC No. 2 Group. It was clear that if the operation was feasible at all, it would fall to the Mosquitoes of this Group.

It was a remarkable twist of fortune that put the fate of the patriots of Amiens into the hands of Basil Embry, for Embry himself owed his life to the French Resistance. On 27 May 1940 he had been shot down during the Battle of France and taken prisoner. Helped by loyal Frenchmen, he had become the first British airman to return home after escaping from the Germans. The prospects for the mounting of an air operation were thus vastly improved.

'I think it might be possible,' Embry said to Coningham, 'but first I'd like to go into it fully. Can I let you know?'

Coningham agreed, and Embry began by getting one of his photographic planes to take pictures of the prison. The plane covered a wide area from a considerable height and aroused no suspicion. The photographs were interpreted, and then the modelling section were asked to produce a replica of the prison, to simulate what the crews might see from about 1000 feet at a distance of four miles. Meanwhile Embry called on the Intelligence Service to provide details of the construction of the prison and its walls, the internal lay-out, the strength of doors and locks, and the general prison routine – all of which had already been supplied by Ponchardier.

The main prison building was cruciform in shape, the long vertical arm lying parallel to the *Route d'Albert*, with the shorter horizontal arm at right angles to it. It was a three-storey building, rising to 66 feet at the gabled intersection of the two arms of the cross. At the base and apex of the vertical arm, nestling under the main building, lay squat extension buildings with corrugated roofing which were known to be the quarters of the German guards. At the left extremity of the horizontal arm lay the main hall and the entrance gates, fronting on to the main road. The right wing of the horizontal arm housed the political prisoners. Surrounding the prison was a rectangular wall, 140 yards long and 110 yards wide, 22 feet high and 3 feet thick.

It was clear that there would be two main tasks – the breaching of the walls, and the opening of the prison. Embry consulted his armaments men on the amount of explosive required, and they warned him that to make sure of these two objectives the quantity of explosive used would be certain to cause casualties amongst the prisoners. Embry passed this warning on to the French Resistance Movement in London. They replied that the prisoners would rather be killed by the bombs of the RAF than by the Germans. Even if only a few were saved, the sacrifice would be worth while.

From all other aspects it was a good target. The town of Amiens gave a perfect pinpoint, and the *Route d'Albert* offered a straight and well-defined lead-in, clear of obstruction to low-level attack. Embry thus felt certain of two things. First, that the operation must be attempted, and secondly, that properly planned and in the right hands it had a fair chance of success. Nevertheless the risk of killing friends and allies weighed heavily on his mind. 'It was a hateful responsibility,' he wrote afterwards.[1]

Embry decided to lead the operation himself. He had never regarded high rank as an automatic disqualification from operational flying, and this was an operation he did not intend to miss. There was no doubt in his mind which formation under his command was best suited to undertake it. The Mosquitoes of 140 Wing, consisting of Nos. 21, 464 (Australian) and 487 (New Zealand) Squadrons, had taken part in many low-level pinpoint operations, notably against the flying-bomb sites. And they were commanded by a man who would be an inspired choice as deputy leader of the operation, a man without peer as a bomber pilot, well-known to the French because of his work on clandestine aerial contacts with Resistance groups, and a man who would never forgive Embry if he were not given the chance to help rescue some of his friends.

[1] In *Mission Completed* (Methuen).

Charles Pickard – 'Pick' – had joined the RAF in 1936. In 1940, as a squadron leader, he had achieved an unwanted fame through his clipped, natural playing of the pilot of Wellington 'F for Freddie' in the film 'Target for Tonight'. After completing a bombing tour he commanded a squadron assisting directly in the dangerous work of subversion and sabotage in France. In February 1942 he led the force of aircraft carrying paratroops in the raid on Bruneval which resulted in the capture of vital German radar secrets. He was now a group captain, commanding a wing, holding the DSO with two bars and the DFC, and with over 100 operational sorties behind him.

Embry, however, had been asked for no more than his opinion. He soon found that most of his seniors disliked the idea of the operation and doubted whether any good purpose would be served by mounting it. Better to let a dozen, twenty, even fifty Resistance men die quietly than to devastate a prison and kill perhaps a hundred people without any real hope of saving life. But Embry was a man ready to fight hard for his beliefs, ready to risk his career rather than submit when he felt sure of his ground. He reiterated his belief that the RAF must answer the call, and he turned the issue into a vote of confidence in his men and aircraft, staking his reputation on success. In the face of such tenacity and confidence his seniors gave in, and Embry instructed his staff to prepare a detailed plan.

On 8 February Embry flew to Hunsden to brief Pickard as deputy leader. The two men agreed that the raid would call for the utmost accuracy and delicacy of judgment, and six crews were specially selected from each of the three squadrons in the wing. Strong fighter protection had been written into the plan. Complete secrecy was to be observed and none of the crews were to be briefed until the day of the operation.

Next day Embry flew to Blackbushe to conduct Leigh-Mallory on an inspection of another wing in his group. As soon as they were alone, Leigh-Mallory asked Embry what progress had been made with Operation 'Jericho'. Embry explained the broad outline of the plan.

'Who's leading it, Basil?' asked Leigh-Mallory.

'I am, sir.'

Mallory nodded, apparently in assent – or so it seemed to Embry. But when Leigh-Mallory got back to his headquarters he changed his mind – if indeed his nod had ever been meant to convey approval. He rang Coningham.

'Hello, Mary. Embry tells me he's put himself down to lead "Jericho".'

'Yes.'

'I'm afraid I must say quite categorically that he is not to fly on this operation – not in any capacity, not in any circumstances. Understood?'

'Yes, sir.'

Coningham passed the ban on to Embry straight away. Embry did his best to wriggle. 'But the briefing's already been done.' This was not quite true – so far he had only briefed Pickard – but it was true that the whole conception of the operation had been his. 'We're all set to go. I can't change the leadership now.'

'I'm sorry,' said Coningham quietly, 'but those are Leigh-Mallory's orders. He was most emphatic about it. I'm afraid you'll just have to accept it.' So the leadership of the operation passed to Pickard.

On 14 February Ponchardier was informed by clandestine radio that a force of Mosquitoes would bomb the prison from low level any day after the 15th. Zero hour would be three minutes after noon. The time had been chosen on the advice of Ponchardier, who knew that the German guards had their lunch at midday. Another factor which influenced him in his choice of time was that there was much coming and going between Amiens and the outlying districts at lunchtime and any prisoners who managed to escape would be less conspicuous then.

But now the weather intervened. Blinding snowstorms grounded all Allied aircraft and soon a blanket of snow covered England and France. Operation 'Jericho' was postponed from day to day.

*     *     *

Inside the jail, Dr Antonin Mans, Public Health Officer and Defence Chief of the Somme Department, stared at the massive lock in the heavy oak door which shut him so securely in his ground-floor cell. He was under sentence of death. The news of a rescue attempt had been smuggled in to him by Ponchardier under the guise of a message from his wife. He could not see how it was to be achieved, but like most of the others he had an immense trust in the skill and courage of the RAF. He had been in Amiens jail since 12 November 1943, caught with almost the entire Amiens group after the treachery of an unknown member. Only one or two whom Mme Mans had been able to warn had managed to escape. All day on the 16 and 17 February he listened for the sound of aircraft engines, but none came. In two days he was to be executed.

Captain André Tempez, regional Resistance leader, was also under sentence of death. So was Jean Beaurin, the twenty-year-old deputy leader of the local *FTPF*, and Maurice Holleville, another leading *FTPF* man.

M. Henri Moisan, a member of the *Organisation Civile et Militaire*, was immured with three other Resistance men in a tiny cell twelve feet by seven on the second floor. Arrested by the Gestapo in August 1942 for suspected complicity in an act of sabotage, he had subsequently been allowed to return to his home in Boulevard Jules Verne, Amiens – the house where the famous writer had died in 1905. But on 26 January 1944 he had been re-arrested and he was now awaiting the inevitable result of a long and bitter interrogation. There was M. Gruel, another member of the Amiens group, now occupying a cell on the first floor formerly occupied by Dr Mans. There was M. Raymond Vivant, *sous-préfet* at Abbeville, only four days previously still in charge of the coastal sector of Somme province, now awaiting a trial whose outcome was certain. There were a hundred others whose lives were at stake.

At noon on 16 and 17 February Ponchardier and a small band of faithful followers patrolled the fields near the jail, keeping hidden as far as possible, seeing without being seen. Ponchardier's main fear now was that news of the proposed attack might leak out. It had been no use keeping the secret to himself – he had had to tell a small army of Resistance men in order to have help ready for the escaping prisoners. It would be pointless to expose them to the hazards of bombing and then leave them to be recaptured. Altogether he thought he must have told over a hundred people. It only needed one informer, or one careless contact, to wreck the whole plan. The Germans would bring the executions forward and the RAF would arrive too late.

But Amiens jail was silent, cloaked in snow. There was no evidence that the Germans were any more on their guard than usual.

And there was no sign, either, of the RAF. They were cutting it fine. On the morning of the 18th Ponchardier decided that if they did not come that day they would not come at all. He thought it quite probable that for political reasons the attack had been called off. He had built his hopes so much on the RAF that he dreaded the passage of time up to midday, fearing the mortal blow to the Resistance if the RAF did not come.

The morning evaporated, and the last minutes up to midday galloped by. At twelve o'clock all Ponchardier's men were in their places, the doubts born of delay written clearly on their faces. The conviction was growing that they had been abandoned. In the next three minutes they would know.

*     *     *

At the RAF airfield at Hunsden the whole station was confined to camp all day on the 16th and 17th, but the weather remained impossible. It was decided to postpone the attack until the 18th, but to make every effort, whatever the weather, to carry it out on that day.

The strain of waiting was beginning to tell, too, on Pickard – the only one of the crews who knew the plan. The Pickard of 1944 was a different man from the Pickard of 1940. Four years of continual operational flying had not changed him fundamentally, but the veneer of the phlegmatically typical Britisher of 'Target for Tonight' had vanished, exposing the real man, tough and resilient, but apt nowadays to be irritable and short-tempered. His task as commander of a wing containing one British and two Commonwealth squadrons was not always easy. The keen competitive spirit sometimes led to complications. And as though this assortment were not enough, Pickard had to contend with the forty-five-year-old French individualist Colonel Philippe Livry-Level (or Squadron Leader Livry, as he was known in the RAF), a patriot who had escaped from France and who was now a navigator on 21 Squadron. The two men had taken part in many clandestine operations together and in spite of frequent differences had a great affection for each other. Indeed they were among the great characters of the war. Together they would discuss a forthcoming operation, with much banter and gesticulation, and then Livry would walk off to join his pilot, the tall, blond 'Buck' Taylor. As he went he would tap the ash off his famous black cigarette-holder in a conclusive gesture, while dozens of maps sprouted and overflowed from the tops of his flying boots. Rumour had it that he used one-inch-to-the-mile maps and navigated by footpaths. Not surprisingly, he was not the easiest man to manage. One example will suffice. Some weeks earlier the wing had been briefed early one morning for a strike against flying-bomb sites in the Pas de Calais. Livry and another officer reached the briefing room first. When Pickard walked in they bade him good morning, but Pickard did not answer. Suddenly he hurled a question at Livry.

'You're not on this trip, are you?'

Livry removed the inevitable long cigarette holder from

the corner of his mouth. 'No sir, zat ees correct.'

'Then what are you doing here?'

'I know ze area well – I came to see if I could help.'

'Why the devil aren't you in bed?'

'Ze bed,' said Livry philosophically, 'ees not made for one.'

Pickard had no answer to this. But another recent incident had upset the wing a good deal. One of the New Zealand pilots, contrary to regulations, had unwisely indulged in aerobatics over the station. Trying something a bit too much for him, he had stalled his Mosquito and crashed into the middle of the camp, killing himself and his navigator and four WAAF parachute packers besides. No one felt the shame of the tragedy more deeply than the New Zealanders, and the incident might have been better left alone. But Pickard could not easily forgive such a shocking piece of flying indiscipline, nor could he forget the death of the four WAAFs. He assembled the crews of the three squadrons and read the riot act. This public rebuke hurt the New Zealanders deeply. They felt they had been kicked when they were down. Pickard himself realised this, and when the final plans for the Amiens raid were drafted he decided to send the New Zealanders in first. This gesture gave them back their self respect.

At eight o'clock on the morning of the 18th, 19 Mosquito crews were called on the Tannoy system to the briefing room. There were six crews from each squadron, plus a single Mosquito of the Film Production Unit. In addition there would be Pickard and his navigator, Flight Lieutenant J. J. ('Bill') Broadley, leading the raid.

It was still snowing heavily and the crews were convinced that no ordinary operation would be attempted in the existing weather. It must be something special. This belief, encouraged by the forty-eight hours' confinement to camp, was reinforced when they got to the briefing room and found a special guard of Service police barring the way. Each man was required to produce his identity card and the names were ticked off a list as they went in.

'What's it all about?' The question was fired at the photographic crew, who generally got an inkling of the target, or at least the type of target, some time before an operation so that they could fit suitable cameras to their aircraft. But this time they had been told very little. 'We shall know when they unveil the statue,' said Flight Lieutenant Tony Wickham, the tall personable photographic pilot. He pointed to a table which stood at the far end of the room.

Everyone stared at a large box which stood on the table. It was about four feet square but shallow, no more than six inches high. It was clearly a model of the target.

The crews huddled round the stove at the side of the room, still numb with cold, fascinated by the box. Soon Pickard came in, followed a moment later by Basil Embry. Pickard took up his position at the table while Embry stood in the background. Behind them, on the far wall, was a map of northern France.

'Your target today,' began Pickard, 'is an exceptional one. I may as well tell you that there's been a lot of talk as to whether it's feasible at all, and the AOC virtually had to ask for a vote of confidence in his crews before we were given the chance of having a crack at it. It can only be attacked successfully by low-flying Mosquitoes, and we've been chosen to do it. We've got to make a big success of it, to justify his faith in us, and to prove once again, if proof is necessary, just how accurately we can put our bombs down.

'The story is this. Here on the table is a model of Amiens jail.' He lifted the model out of its box and displayed it for all to see. 'Inside this prison are more than a hundred French patriots who have been condemned to death, or who will be condemned to death, for assisting the Allies. Some of them have been condemned for helping airmen like ourselves to escape after being brought down in France. Some of the executions are imminent. The prison is surrounded by a wall over twenty feet high. It is well guarded. There is no conceivable ground operation which could help these prisoners to escape. Only by breaking down the prison walls with our bombs, and smashing the exterior walls of the prison itself, can we give our friends any reasonable chance of escape.

'That is what we are going to have a crack at today. We're going to bust that prison wide open.

'There are six crews detailed from each of the three squadrons, and we shall have three squadrons of Typhoons as escort. In addition the RAF Film Unit's special Mosquito is coming along to see what sort of a job we make of it.

'I want you to study the model of the jail in detail after the briefing. You will see that the prison lies to the northeast of Amiens, outside the town and in open country on the road to Albert. This long, straight road gives us an excellent lead-in.' Pickard then described the construction of the prison and its surrounding wall. 'Six aircraft of 487 Squadron,' he went on, 'will lead the raid, their task being to breach the outer wall in two places. They will be split into two sections of three. The first section will run straight in along the *Route d'Albert* and attack the east wall here.' He pointed to the wall at the base of the cross. 'The second section will break away to starboard four miles from the target at sufficient height to watch the attack of the first section. When the bombs of the first section have gone off, the second section will attack the north wall on a north–south run. That will give us our two breaches.

'It's essential to breach two sides of the wall in this way. Breaches in the wall on one side only might give the German guards a chance to seal off that side of the prison, but with two walls smashed that should be impossible.

'To drop your bombs fair and square into these walls is going to mean some real low-level flying, right down on the deck. If we're not damned careful our bombs are going to sail over the top, or perhaps bounce over the top, in which case they'll land inside the prison and blow everyone to smithereens. We've got to cut that risk down to a minimum. We've got to be below the height of the wall when we let go. That means getting down to ten or fifteen feet. There are no obstructions on the run in so we should be able to make it.

'Note that accurate timing is essential if we're going to avoid blowing each other up with our own bombs.

'Now we come to the second six, of 464 Squadron, again split into two sections of three. Your task is to lay your bombs against the walls of the main prison building. This is the most delicate task of all.'

Pickard paused for a moment, and then pointed to the two corrugated annexes at the base and apex of the cross. 'These two low extension buildings are the quarters of the German guards. They are built right in the shadow of the prison, using the main prison wall as support. You are to bomb these two annexes, using a section of three aircraft for each annex. In doing so you will severely damage the main prison wall and shake every door off its hinges and every lock out of its hasp.

'Again you must watch your timing so that you don't fly into the blast of each other's bombs.

'The film aircraft will follow this second formation and will orbit the target, filming the result of the raid.' Pickard turned to Wickham. 'We're dropping eleven-second delay bombs, as you know,' he said. 'You'll have to lose a minute or so near the target to give the bombs a chance to go off before you make your first run over the prison.' Wickham nodded.

'The first six aircraft will be on target at three minutes past twelve. The second six will attack three minutes later.

'The last six aircraft, of 21 Squadron, will hold off until ten minutes after this second attack. Their task will depend entirely on the success or failure of the first two squadrons. They will only attack objectives that have not been destroyed by the first two waves. If the job has been done they will pass north of Amiens and set course for home without dropping their bombs.'

Wing Commander 'Daddy' Dale, thirty-eight-year-old commander of 21 Squadron, got to his feet. Already the disappointing news that his squadron was to go in last, and might not go in at all, had squeezed from him his favourite expression, in a whispered aside, 'Fan me with a plate of soup.' Now he addressed Pickard, 'Who will decide whether the attack is a success or not, sir?'

'I shall be flying at the end of the second wave,' said Pickard. 'When I've dropped my bombs I shall pull off to the north of the prison and circle. I shall have a good view of the second wave's attack as I run in, and when the smoke has cleared I shall be able to evaluate the whole attack. I shall signal to the last wave by radio. We'll use the signals 'red' and 'green', repeated three times. So if you hear me say 'red, red, red', you'll know that you're being warned off. If I say 'green, green, green', then it's all clear for you to go in and bomb.

'As an additional precaution, in case I have a radio failure or something of that sort, the film aircraft will have just as good a view of the whole show, so he can act as cover for me. I'll discuss that with Wickham in a moment. If you get no signal from me, you'll get a red or a green from Wickham.'

For the next hour the crews studied the model and checked and counter-checked their routes and timings. Embry left them to it. At ten o'clock hot tea was brought round. Meanwhile Pickard put a final call through to group headquarters.

'It's still snowing over south-eastern England,' he told the crews when he came off the phone, 'and the visibility's bad, but I think we can get off the deck all right, and the weather may improve across the Channel. I've just had a word with Group and they're talking about postponing again for 24 hours. I told them I thought another postponement was unthinkable, and they've left the final decision to us.'

The chorus of dissent at the first hint of a postponement had already convinced Pickard. The crews were determined to go, and there was nothing more to be said.

The air situation at this time – three and a half months before the invasion – was that to fly over France at low level in daylight, even in a Mosquito, was not a healthy occupation. To linger over the target, as Pickard and Wickham would be doing, multiplied the hazards many times. But the fighter escort would keep an eye on them.

At half-past ten the twenty Mosquitoes lined up at the bottom of the runway in readiness for a prompt take-off at eleven. The pilots switched off and the crews got out to stretch their legs. Excitement and cold combined to shiver limbs and to weaken bladders, and the crews congregated at the rear of their planes. 'A man daren't even drink a cup of tea in this weather,' joked Pickard.

A eleven o'clock the first Mosquito, flown by Wing Commander 'Black' Smith, the hirsute commanding officer of the New Zealand squadron, moved off down the snow-caked runway, churning up a fine powder of snow. All the Mosquitoes got off safely and formed up in threes before setting course for the rendezvous with the fighters at Littlehampton.

Almost at once both the Mosquitoes and the Typhoons ran into blinding snowstorms. Four Mosquitoes lost the formation on the way down to Littlehampton and failed to keep the rendezvous with the fighters, and after a fruitless chase turned back to Hunsden. And the Typhoons, taking off from Manston and Westhampnett to converge on Littlehampton, ran into ten-tenths low cloud and the same opaque snowstorms and soon got split up. Of the twelve Typhoons that took off, only eight met the Mosquitoes at Littlehampton.

Over the Channel the snowstorms thinned out a little and visibility improved. Soon the formation was sweeping over the water at zero feet, exulting in the thrill of low flying. Approaching the French coast they pulled up to 5000 feet, crossed the coastline ten miles north-east of Dieppe, and then dived down again to race at 250 miles an hour low across the snow-carpeted French countryside. All the way the Typhoons stayed with them, tied to the wing-tips of the outside men.

Map-reading at low-level over snow-covered ground was

difficult and at first the leading Mosquitoes missed Amiens. They orbited twice before altering course, swinging round north of Amiens and back to hit the road to Albert. 'Black' Smith, leading the first section, pushed the nose of his Mossie forward until he was hurtling along parallel with the road, just missing the black telegraph poles that stood out like the spikes of a rake.

So far the pilots had kept fairly loose formation, but now they closed up wing-tip to wing-tip to concentrate their bombing, charging towards the right-hand end of the east wall of the prison, now clearly visible less than a mile ahead. Behind Smith the two remaining Mosquitoes of the second section – one had lost the formation on the way to Little-hampton – swung northwards in a wide arc, turning back just in time to watch the first attack.

The prison itself was rearing above them when Smith and the leading section dropped their bombs, aimed at the base of the walls. All three pilots pulled up and shot across the prison, the roar of their engines shattering the noonday routine. As they pulled away, the two pilots attacking the wall from the north were settling down on their bombing run.

These two pilots, and the leading section of the Australian squadron, had a grandstand view of Smith's attack. They saw to their astonishment that the bombs of Smith's section had shot straight through or over the eastern wall and careered across the courtyard before crashing into the wall on the far side – the western wall – where a few seconds later they exploded. Not all the bombs had crossed the court-yard unimpeded, however. One had struck the main prison building.

The two Mosquitoes attacking the northern wall from the north aimed for the right-hand end and hit it. At the junc-tion of the northern and western wall, whole chunks of brickwork collapsed, showing up black against the snow. Again a single bomb hit the main prison building.

Both the stray bombs had hit the northern horizontal arm

of the cross. This was the section where the political prisoners were housed.

Now came the two Australian sections to bomb the German guards. The bad weather at the start of the operation had reduced each section to two aircraft only. Leading the first section was Wing Commander Bob Iredale, the fair, balding squadron CO. From four miles away he saw the prison and the first three aircraft pulling up against the skyline after dropping their bombs. He could see no breach in the eastern wall, and he decided to bomb it. A slight overshoot by one bomb would take care of the guards' quarters at the base of the cross as well.

When he was about 400 yards from the prison the bombs of the New Zealand section went off and he saw that they had breached the far wall, also the north wall to the right. Then everything at the western end of the prison was obscured in thick smoke and dust. He swept in towards the eastern wall at fifty feet, overshot slightly, and scored a direct hit on the quarters of the guards. Meanwhile the other Australian section had broken off and swept round from the north to attack the corrugated annex at the apex of the cross. They scored direct hits and demolished the building.

\*　　　\*　　　\*

Inside the jail, the scenes were comparable only to earthquake or volcanic shock. The distant wail of the sirens in Amiens was soon drowned by the roaring reverberations of aircraft engines, colliding and ricocheting round the prison buildings, and the crump and shock of falling bombs. These alone rocked the walls of the prison and sent a turbulence of agitated air down the icy corridors and rattled the cell doors. But this was only the harmless beginning. So far the bombs had not gone off.

Every prisoner climbed on to his bed and stood on tiptoe trying to see out of the tiny apertures in each cell that served as windows. Some sort of air battle was obviously going on overhead but only the privileged few had any idea

185

what it was. Then, when the noise of the planes had receded and the shock of falling bombs subsided, the prison seemed to belch and regurgitate the high explosive as though tormented by a mighty cataclysm from within. Walls disintegrated, floors collapsed, cell doors were flung open, and the terrified prisoners stared helplessly through shattered brickwork at the open sky. Scores were killed in the first attack, many writhed on the floors of their cells in agony.

The next hazard was dust – clouds of choking, suffocating dust which permeated every cell and blinded the prisoners as they groped around their crumbling cells for a way of escape. The same heavy suspension of dust baffled Ponchardier and his group of rescuers, together with many nearby villagers who dashed in through gaps in the wall to aid the prisoners.

On the second floor, Henri Moisan was lying on his bunk reading and awaiting the midday distribution of soup. He jumped up at the sound of aircraft engines and through the high cell window saw a khaki-camouflaged Mosquito flash by at rooftop level. In the same instant the first explosion blew in all the windows throughout the prison. Moisan and the other occupants of his cell shrank back towards the door. Several more violent explosions followed and Moisan sensed that he was falling, and with him a great quantity of masonry and prison fittings. His fall ended on the floor below, where he lay badly injured but still conscious, completely buried by debris and overwhelmed with shock. He was rescued by another prisoner, Louis Sellier, who abandoned his own chance of escape to save Moisan.

On the first floor, the twenty-year-old Jean Beaurin of the *FTPF*, together with the three other men in his cell, was thrown to the floor again and again by successive explosions. The four men kicked open the half-unhinged cell door and emerged on to the landing to survey a scene of frightful devastation. Beaurin's brother had been killed and his mother wounded, but he could not find them. He was joined by his comrade Maurice Holleville and together they made a dash for the breached wall. M. Gruel, of the Amiens group, like many others, had been killed in his cell – the cell occupied until recently by Dr Mans.

Dr Mans, on the ground floor, was one of the first to get clear of the prison building. Stunned by the explosions, he found that his desire to escape had gone. All that remained was the vague knowledge that it was his duty to do so if he could. He staggered through the wrecked hall and out into the courtyard. Almost at once he heard someone calling his name.

'Dr Mans!'

It was Captain Tempez, calling to him from his first floor cell. He went back into the building, found a key in the smashed Gestapo offices, and clambered up the twisted iron staircase. He opened the door of Tempez' cell. Other prisoners whose cell doors had not been blown open were clamouring to be released and someone grabbed the key from his hand and rushed on down the corridor.

Behind the shouts of those still imprisoned lay the muted groans of the wounded, the maimed and the dying. Still following his instinct, Dr Mans closed his mind to these heart-rending cries. He slid down the iron supports of the mangled staircase and emerged into the courtyard.

On the ground in front of him lay a woman, her legs severed at the thigh. Her husband was on the ground beside her, cushioning her head. Dr Mans was compelled to stop in front of them.

It was his duty to escape. It was his duty to the Resistance, it was his duty to France. It wasn't just a question of saving his own life. The whole Resistance organisation would collapse if the leaders failed to escape. Only by regaining their freedom and consulting together could they ever hope to uncover the informer and fight back. But wasn't there another duty, a duty to one's fellow men? Was it a mistake to think that this was a wider duty, the duty to humanity, without which all resistance to evil was meaningless?

He knelt down beside the woman. There was little he

could do for her. He heard Tempez calling behind him.

'What are you going to do, Dr Mans?'

'I'm staying. I shall do what I can for the injured.'

'Then I shall stay with you.'

Several other Frenchmen under sentence of death joined Mans and Tempez in the rescue work. Helpers from outside pleaded with them to go but they refused. The work of mercy was not halted by racial barriers. Many of the guards had been wounded and they too were treated by Dr Mans and his party.

Ponchardier and his followers, and the people of the village, stayed within the prison walls until 12.15, by which time over 400 prisoners had escaped. Then they dispersed as quickly and quietly as possible. The Germans did not arrive in strength for some time.

*     *     *

Above the prison, the Film Production Unit Mosquito circled from 12.03 to 12.10, taking a ciné-film of the attack. At the insistence of his cameraman, stretched out in the nose, Tony Wickham made three separate slow runs smack across the target. Pickard, too, was circling at 500 feet, assessing the results of the bombing so far, while the Typhoons figure-skated in and out, driving off a formation of FW 190s that had suddenly appeared in the general mêlée. Both Pickard and Wickham could see clusters of dungareed prisoners emerging into the courtyard near the workshops. The first three pygmy figures were already escaping through the hole in the north wall and making off across the snow.

A thick pall of smoke was drifting over the western half of the prison and out across the west wall, smoothed and flattened by the east wind. Wickham turned away in a tight left-hand circuit and called his cameraman.

'Can we go now?' ·

'Let's have just one more.'

'Here we go, then.'

This time they discovered how to distinguish the prisoners

from the guards. As they flew over the prison, the guards flung themselves flat on their faces. The prisoners kept on running.

Several of the attacking aircraft and their escort had been hit and FW 190s were still shooting around the target perimeter. But Pickard was satisfied that the operation had gone well. The smoke obscured much of the damage, but he could see that the destruction had been considerable, and he decided to call off the attack by 21 Squadron. Large numbers of prisoners were still escaping and any further attack might do more harm than good. He called up 21 Squadron.

'Daddy from Dypeg. Daddy from Dypeg. Red, red, red.'

'Well, fan me with a plate of soup,' said 'Daddy' Dale. It was disappointing after coming all this way, but it was a relief to know that the job had been well and truly done. He led his squadron back to Hunsden.

Squadron Leader McRitchie, leader of the second Australian section, was hit by anti-aircraft fire near Albert as the squadron tried to re-form. He quickly lost height but managed to keep on course for a time. Then the starboard wing dropped ominously and the Mosquito spiralled earthwards. McRitchie survived the crash and was taken prisoner, but his navigator, Flight Lieutenant Sampson, was killed. Sampson was one of two brothers, both over normal aircrew age, who had sold their farm in New Zealand at the outbreak of war to join the RAF. Both were killed in action.

Pickard saw McRitchie's Mosquito in trouble near Albert and when the raid was over he set off in a north-easterly direction to investigate. All the other Mosquitoes, together with the fighter escort, turned north-west. A minute or so later, a farmer at Montigny saw a lone Mosquito, apparently already damaged by small-arms fire, appear from the direction of Amiens. The fuselage was boldly marked with a capital F. He saw, too, that a single-engined aircraft was giving chase. As it passed him he saw the black cross on the fuselage and recognised the sawn-off wings of an FW 190.

The German fighter quickly closed on the Mosquito's tail. There was a burst of fire, and then the farmer saw part of the Mosquito's tail fall away. Immediately afterwards the Mosquito spun in.

The farmer had witnessed the end of one of the great airmen of the war, a man whose face and personality had been known to millions through the filmed exploits of 'F for Freddie', but who now lay dead amongst the snows of Picardy. With him died Bill Broadley, who had flown with Pickard since the early days of the war, earning the DSO, the DFC, and the DFM. Broadley had unselfishly continued as Pickard's navigator when there had been many opportunities for promotion elsewhere.

There were losses, too, amongst the fighter escort. A Canadian pilot was shot down near the target and made a safe forced landing. Another pilot, his aircraft damaged during the action, continued to provide close escort until the formation hit bad weather in the Channel. He was last seen climbing into thick snow cloud some twenty miles south of Beachy Head.

\*　　　\*　　　\*

Back in Amiens, the Germans were beginning the vigorous prosecution of search and interrogation. The work of Dr Mans impressed them and he and his helpers were promised a pardon. For the moment the Germans were more interested in hunting down the escapers. Many of the men under sentence had been confronted with Gestapo agents at their trial and the identification of these agents would be of incalculable value to the whole Resistance organisation.

A good many of the escapers were recaptured, and others, fearing reprisals against their families, gave themselves up, so that when the profit and loss account for the raid came to be calculated after the Liberation it was found that of the 400-odd escapers only about 250 had retained their freedom. 102 prisoners had been killed in the attack and 74 wounded, some of them by small-arms fire from the guards. So it was inevitable that many people, French and British, should ask themselves, both at the time and later, whether the raid should have been asked for, and having been asked for, whether it should have been carried out.

Rémy, one of the foremost Resistance leaders, has confessed[1] that his first reaction was that it would have been better if Ponchardier had never conceived the idea at all. But he then puts forward three convincing reasons why such an initial reaction was utterly wrong. The first was that the objective of the operation – to release key Resistance men who were either under sentence of death or who would most certainly be condemned to death – was substantially achieved. Secondly, the identification of Gestapo agents by the escapers – including some of those who were later recaptured – undermined German counter-espionage throughout the Somme region. Thirdly, and most important of all, Britain had kept faith with the clandestine armies of the Maquis. It was heartbreaking to think of the loss of innocent lives – men and women held for minor offences whose release within a few weeks would have been automatic – but these, too, had died for France.

At first the people of Amiens were puzzled and resentful. They could not understand why it was that the wing occupied by the political prisoners should have been the most severely damaged. It almost looked as though an attempt had been made to wipe out these men for fear that they might talk. But when, within two or three days, it was learned that M. Raymond Vivant, *sous-préfet* of Abbeville and the most important Frenchman in the jail, and twelve Resistance leaders who would otherwise have been shot within forty-eight hours, were among the escapers, their bitterness evaporated and they applauded the success of the raid.

On 23 February, five days after the raid, a message was received in England from the French underground. 'I thank you in the name of our comrades,' it began, 'for the bom-

[1] In *The Gates Burst Open* (Arco).

bardment of the prison. Thanks to the admirable precision of the attack the first bombs blew in nearly all the doors, and with the help of the civilian population some 150[1] prisoners made good their escape. Twelve of these were to have been shot next day. The bombing was too violent – thirty-seven prisoners were killed, some of them by German machine-guns. Fifty Germans were also killed. To sum up it was a success.' The message added the opinion that the delayed action of the bombs should have been longer : few prisoners had time to take what cover they could before the bombs went off.

In retrospect it does seem that the attack was too heavy, even though only nine of the first twelve aircraft reached their objective and the last wave was called off. But much of the loss of life amongst the prisoners was almost certainly caused by bombs aimed at the walls, bombs which crashed through the walls and careered on. In any case it was very difficult to drop a bomb from low level into a 20-foot wall and then clear a 60-foot high building immediately beyond it. Some of the bombs were probably dropped well before the wall, in which case they may have bounced over the top; or they were dropped too late, when the pilot was almost in the act of climbing to clear the wall and the prison behind it, and were thus propelled clean over the wall, landing beyond it.

Four aircraft dropped their bombs at the east wall, yet photographs taken during and after the raid show little or no damage to this wall. Some of these bombs were actually seen to cross the prison courtyard and hit the western wall 140 yards away. Others hit the north wing where the political prisoners were housed.

But these hazards were known and inescapable. They were accepted – indeed, demanded – by the French. It was no good being squeamish. It was inherent in the conception of the operation that lives could only be saved at the cost of

[1] For obvious reasons the correct figures were not known outside the jail.

lives sacrificed.

Taking a longer view, the effect of the operation on the morale of the Resistance forces was not fully appreciated until D-Day. 'News of this great endeavour on the part of the RAF,' wrote Rémy later, 'spread swiftly through the ranks of the Resistance movement, giving the men new courage and the will to be ready to do all they could on the eve of the landings.' As with so much Allied bombing, it was the imponderables which counted most in the end.

In his D-Day despatch General Eisenhower paid a just tribute to the work of the Resistance. 'Special mention must be made,' he said, 'of the great assistance given us by the French Forces of the Interior. . . .' Without this support, not simply on D-Day but in the months preceding it, the invasion might have been delayed many months and would certainly have cost many more British, American and Allied lives when it came.

What happened to the men who stayed behind in Amiens jail, men like Dr Mans and Captain Tempez? Did the Germans keep their promise?

Unfortunately it cannot be said that they did. After Arras was liberated in October 1944, 260 bodies were found buried outside the town. Among them were most of the Amiens prisoners who had deliberately stayed behind to take part in the work of mercy. Captain Tempez was among them. They had been shot in April 1944, two months after the Mosquito attack.

Moisan was more fortunate. Covered in bloodstains and dust and with his clothes torn to shreds he was taken for dead by the Germans, but his friend Sellier got him on to a stretcher, and the *Défense Passive* took him away in an ambulance, ostensibly to hospital but actually to the house of his brother-in-law, who was a doctor. He recovered and was eventually liberated by the advancing British armies.

Dr Mans, too, survived. Many of the German guards owed their lives to him, and somehow his life was spared. He was eventually deported to Germany, where he spent the winter of 1944–5 in the labour camp at Fallersleben under conditions of the utmost misery and degradation. Many of the prisoners died before the Americans liberated the survivors on 2nd May 1945. As the Americans entered the camp a young Resistance hero, scarcely more than a boy, lay dying from malnutrition and exposure in Dr Mans' arms. 'It was to save the prisoners from a fate like this,' wrote Rémy later, 'that Operation Jericho took place.' And, he might have added, from a fate like that of Captain Tempez. The exposure of these brutalities after the war did much to convince the doubters that the operation was justified.

Dr Mans later presented the lock from the door of his cell at Amiens to the Imperial War Museum as a personal tribute to Charles Pickard, to whom he considered he owed his life.

The bombing of Amiens jail remains one of the most poignant and desperate military operations ever undertaken. In spite of the terrible loss of life it created a bond between two nations which will not easily be forgotten. And the lives it cost were given in the greatest of all national causes – the liberation of the homeland.

Today the name of Pickard, Pickard of Picardy, cannot be spoken in France without emotion.

# SOME AFTERTHOUGHTS – Forty Years On

## Chapter 1 – Daylight Over Augsburg

The briefing officers at the bomber bases of Waddington and Woodhall Spa, Lincolnshire, on 17th April, 1942, left their assembled audiences in no doubt what was expected of them.

"Bomber Command have come up with a real beauty this time," was the warning preamble by the wing commander at Woodhall Spa.

The speaker at Waddington – Squadron Leader "Babe" Learoyd, already himself the hero of a famous raid of the previous year – spelt it out for them even more pointedly. "I shan't be coming with you. I've got my VC already. I've no desire to get another."

As a group, these men were the cream of Bomber Command, and their combined reminiscences are unique. Nearly all were on their second tour. An exception was the raid leader, Squadron Leader John Nettleton, a South African. Promoted on the squadron, he was one of the first to fly the Lancaster.

The target that day, in the heart of Bavaria, was the M.A.N. diesel-engine works at Augsburg (Maschinenfabrik Augsburg Nurnberg A.G.), reputed to be the largest factory of its kind in Germany, producing half the total requirement for the larger submarines then in production.

It so happened that Britain had just acquired a new and formidable weapon, not yet fully tested in combat: the four-engined Avro Lancaster bomber. Might it not perhaps be applied here?

The degree of success of Bomber Command in two and a half years of war so far, despite the dogged persistence of its crews, had been lamentable. Costly attempts to bomb enemy territory in daylight had soon obliged them to seek the cover of darkness. Yet a statistical analysis of night photographs (the Butt Report, August 1941), taken by the bomber crews themselves, showed that in raids over the Ruhr, where many of the major targets were situated, not one bomb in ten fell within five miles of its target.

The much-vaunted bombing of Germany, to "Give it 'em back", as was often said, following the blitz on Britain's cities, was a sick joke. The recent introduction of new radar aids promised radical improvement: but how much greater might the promise be with the new Lancaster?

How a tragic chance encounter with Luftwaffe fighters left 49 of the 85 Lancaster crewmen missing believed killed when the day ended is told here, thanks to the vivid recall of survivors. Sadly, not all those 36 lucky men survived the war. Fewer still survive today.

None of these men were to receive the campaign medal that "Bomber" Harris sought for them. But all but one of the survivors were ready to talk exhaustively about their role. The exception was the raid leader's second pilot, Patrick Dorehill. "Now, twenty years after the war started, I believe it is time we forgot about it," he wrote. "I hope you will forgive me, therefore, if I do not co-operate."

Yet he had already had a poignant insight into the German side of the story when he wrote. He was one of the many surviving wartime Lancaster pilots whose skills found employment in civil aviation after the war. "Flying into Schwechat (the airport for Vienna) in 1948," he recalled, "I happened to be up in the control tower filing my return flight plan when an Austrian, about my own age, asked me what I flew during the war, and when I told him Hampdens and Lancasters he remarked that he had come up against the latter. When I showed some interest and he went into detail, imagine our surprise to find that we had actually opposed each other that very afternoon. He had been awarded the Iron Cross for his very daring achievement in shooting two of our aircraft down."

It had, as we had thought, been a chance encounter. "About a dozen of my mates were returning to our base in France when we saw you roaring past our field at low level and we gave chase."

Dorehill added: "I'm afraid the .303 Brownings of the Lancasters were no match for the cannon shells of the Messerschmitts."

Chance encounter or not, the débâcle only confirmed Harris' prejudice against what he called "panacea" targets, and strengthened his resolve to pursue his appointed wartime task of the area bombing of Germany.

## Chapter 2 – The Highlander

In titling the second story *The Highlander*, I was taken to task for making the erroneous assumption that Kinross is in the Highlands. Again I was fortunate in having detailed accounts from the surviving crew, who all spoke of George Thompson's selfless conduct. I also had a letter from George's father stressing his son's membership, before enlistment, of the Kinross branch of the Red Cross and of the Home Guard. "Very happy in his work as a certificated grocer, he was particularly kind to elderly people. Many a ration book he helped old folks to fill in." He added: "Please note I do not wish my name to be published." Selfless again, like father, like son.

On Monday 6th July, 1970, five survivors of George Thompson's crew, by this time middle-aged, met at their old base of RAF Waddington, among them pilot Harry Denton from New Zealand, to remember the two crewmen lost and to celebrate their own survival years.

A letter from Gwen Potts, widow of Taffy Potts, the daddy of the crew, the only other casualty – and the only married man – was a stark reminder. She told – without evident bitterness – of her husband's volunteering for flying duties although exempt from war service, and of her only child Christine, born two months to the day before her father's death. "On our next leave," the navigator, Ted Kneebone, from Manchester, remembered promising, "We were all going to his home to wet the baby's head." Gwen Potts went on to echo the sentiments of many a young wife left with a small child in this way. "I don't know what I'd have done without her."

The same experience is recorded by the widow of an Augsburg crewman, though with an undertone of resentment. On reading Chapter 1 she wrote: "As a sequel, I could write an article which would present the other side of the picture, that of those who had to be told the news – in this case, with a child expected the following September...."

Most of these chapters originally appeared at various times in a Sunday newspaper under the working title *Heroes of the Bombers*. The correspondence they inspired was not always congratulatory. Reminders of the reverse side of the coin didn't come only from the bereaved. "Heroes of the Bombers? I was one of them."

That was the reaction of a wartime flight engineer. He had been through the bad times, the empty beds, the loss of friends, the disappearance of apparent indestructables, the LMF (lack of moral fibre), the desperate attempts at rallying the troops. "I can remember the Secretary of State for Air" (he called him the Minister for Air), "Sir Archibald Sinclair," (he got the name right) "visiting us at RAF Waddington in late 1942, when there was a lot of talk about strikes among aircrew."

Waddington was the base which lost so many men at Augsburg, also the base from which Middleton and his crew flew on New Year's Day 1943. This was serious, stressed the letter. The Minister came to boost morale.

"His words, as he paced the crew room, still ring in my mind. 'England will never forget you, Britain thanks you etc. etc.'." These extravagant promises went on and on. He adds: "They were indeed strange days."

Stranger still, perhaps, that by 1961, now 52, married with two children, the writer had been made redundant, was on National Assistance, and was "pestering" the Assistance Board for his post-war credits. Did I know a Government Department with enough clout to get him those credits so he could pay off his debts? He signed himself (after his surname) ex-Squadron Leader, DFC.

## Chapter 3 – The Maastricht Bridges

The mass raids of the later war years were mounted mostly by men who had enlisted for the duration and who after the war would go back to their civilian trade or profession. Such raids have tended to obscure the memory of the small pinpoint bombing attacks of the first few months of the war, mounted by an élite band of professional airmen using obsolete weapons from a bygone era. Yet some of these raids demanded a skill, aggression and readiness for sacrifice scarcely exceeded in the years that followed. Such a raid was the one by volunteer crews of No. 12 Squadron on the bridges over the Albert Canal at Maastricht, Belgium on 12th May 1940.

For leading a section of this raid at low level, and leaving an indelible mark, two regular airmen, Pilot Officer Donald Garland (inevitably "Judy"), and Sergeant Tom Gray (inevitably "Dolly"), were posthumously awarded the Victoria Cross. My subsequent reconstruction, including an eye-witness account by another section leader (taken prisoner), brought a sharp protest from a surviving gunner, Basil Carey, who also went on the raid.

"I have always felt" he wrote "that a grievous mistake was made in that, although both Garland and Gray may have earned their VCs, if they did, then why was the award withheld from the third member of their crew, a wireless operator/air gunner, whose name I have forgotten or, since I was a fairly newcomer to the squadron, probably never knew. I know there was a third member."

Basil Carey is right. There was a third member. He too was a regular airman, a non-commissioned rear gunner, LAC L. R. Reynolds – Lawrence Royston Reynolds, generally known as "Roy". He is buried with the rest of his crew in the War Graves Commission Cemetery at Haverlee, Belgium. And in fact he is not wholly forgotten: he was mentioned in despatches.

I am indebted to my friend Chaz Bowyer (*For Valour, The Air VCs*) for fuller details of Garland's and Gray's service careers. Dr. C. J. Garland, CMG, and his wife Renee, lost all their four boys to the RAF, three killed and one died on active service. And incredibly, Gray, the fourth-born of seven brothers, five of whom joined the air force, and three of whom, like Tom, became "Trenchard Brats" (aircraft apprentices), was one of three of the five who died while flying with the RAF.

One more word about Roy Reynolds. A poignant postscript from the *RAF Short History* (HMSO) is quoted on Page 74, as an answer to Basil Carey's lament.

## Chapter 4 – Hughie Edwards

Hughie Edwards, of No. 105 (Blenheim) Squadron, of the No. 2 Group light bomber low-level force, was leader of a spectacular daylight raid on Bremen in June 1941, planned as a reaction to Hitler's attack on Russia, to remind him of his liabilities at home, and to demonstrate Britain's solidarity with her new allies.

The only feasible way such raids could help Russia, convince them of our sincerity, and (all-importantly) help to keep them in the war, lay in the long-term diversion of enemy resources, from external aggression to the defence of the homeland. Over a period it was to contribute decisively.

Churchill, in a retaliatory call to arms at this time, forecast a bombing offensive aimed specifically at "making the German people taste and gulp each month a sharper dose of the miseries they have showered upon mankind." Achievement so far had been modest, but the intention was clear.

Edwards, an Australian in the RAF, and a photogenic six-footer, was known fondly by his ground crews as "The Wingco". Of heroic mould, Edwards and 105 were given the pivotal role, after the leader of their sister squadron, No. 107 (based nearby), Laurence Petley (Petters), had abandoned a similar raid two days earlier for lack of cloud cover. A young pilot officer named W. J. (Bill) Edrich, who was No. 2 to Petley on this abortive raid, was critical of the decision to replace Petley, and has since described the scene back at base when Petley had to endure a "rocket" on the phone from the Air Officer Commanding, Air Commodore D. F. Stevenson. This was in front of the whole squadron, with a clear implication of cowardice. Petley, a gallant but normally reticent officer, exploded: "If that's what you think, Sir, we'll do the whole bloody show again this afternoon."

That chance was denied him, and next day Edwards replaced him. The contrast between the fate of the two leaders was to prove extreme. Petters, unjustly demoted, was shot down and killed with his crew. Edwards, finishing the war with the VC, KCMG, CB, DSO, OBE, and DFC, was to become the most highly decorated of all Australians.

At the time I had a younger brother, rejected as aircrew through colour-blindness (a disqualification in those days), to whom, with his colleagues as fitters and riggers, Edwards was the godlike "Wingco". As it happened I got to know Hughie Edwards personally after the war, playing cricket for an RAF side, and although he still limped noticeably from a pre-war flying injury, I know that, as an Australian, he loved to play. Surely, I thought, there must have been a station XI at Swanton Morley? There certainly was at Bill Edrich's base nearby. But my brother Paul, no mean cricketer himself, does not remember there being one at Swanton Morley. All East Anglian bases of No. 2 Group, he reminds me, were then under daily bombardment – or the threat of it – from tip and run raiders from an ascendant Luftwaffe, and the casualties inflicted, in the air especially, were insupportably high. "Everything was rather serious about those times," says Paul. Remembering the decimating 2 Group losses of that period, this must stand as a masterpiece of understatement.

## Chapter 5 – The Outback Aussie

The central figure in this story was also Australian, but totally different from the glamorous Edwards. Rawdon Hume (Ron) Middleton was an introspective, even melancholic 26-year-old, naïve, perhaps, but mature enough to wonder what he was doing such a long way from home, brooding on the role assigned to him – the long-range bombing of a people with whom, as an Australian, he had no territorial quarrel. Descended from an 1820 immigrant of impeccable pedigree – the Reverend G. A. Middleton, a Cambridge graduate – he found himself training with a polyglot miscellany of humanity, keen enough to fight but not easy to weld into a crew. Yet the loyalty, dedication and devotion to each other that developed – typical qualities of wartime aircrew – were never better exemplified than with this disparate collection – among them a student, a garage hand, and a Scottish gamekeeper.

Perhaps, like the bombed-out citizens of London, Middleton grew in resentment with enemy goading: he was second pilot in a Stirling which limped home all but mortally crippled by night fighters and flak. A narrow escape, but a galvanising one. When, soon afterwards, Middleton was told by the great Pathfinder recruiter, Hamish Mahaddie, that he was to be transferred to PFF, minus one or two of his crew, who weren't up to scratch, Middleton rebelled. He would stick with his crew. How he repaid them is told here.

Incidentally, one of Ron Middleton's crew, the Scottish

gamekeeper, Doug Cameron, was later to achieve a unique distinction. For a second time, he was to be a survivor of a crew in which the pilot won a posthumous VC.

## Chapter 6 – Guy Gibson

Guy Gibson's restless urge to resume operational flying – it was an occupational disease or hazard, driving many men to seek a return to a vulnerability and comradeship they could not live without – is confirmed by "Bomber" Harris himself, who found Gibson's oft-repeated pleas finally irresistible, as did his group commander, Sir Ralph Cochrane, who adds: "The attack on Rheydt in which Gibson acted as Master Bomber was his first since the raid on the Dams." There were in fact one or two minor exceptions, but this does appear to have been *his first major assignment* since that time.

"He was given permission to take part," says Sir Ralph, "because the target was close to the Allied lines, and he successfully completed the direction of the attack, as we know, but was shot down near the Dutch coast on the way home."

Gibson, as pilot of the two-man crew of a Pathfinder Mosquito, had as his navigator the 23-year-old Squadron Leader J. B. (James Brown) Warwick, DFC, an Irishman, Paddy to his friends. He was a veteran of two bomber tours. (Gibson himself was still only 26). Nevertheless it has to be said that neither man, experienced as they were, was in current practice for the role.

I am indebted to a Dutch researcher and friend, Gerrit J. Zwanenburg, for much of the detail of Gibson's last flight and resting place, and indeed of many other men of Bomber Command who crashed in the Netherlands, mostly on their way home. I have had his help in tracing casualties for over 40 years. Also in 1961, via the current Burgomaster, I received a detailed summary of the incident, dated 21st September 1944, the day after the raid. The summary was signed by a former Deputy-Mayor of Steenbergen (his boss, a Nazi, with the Allies at that time close at hand, had already fled). Although the identity of James Warwick was confirmed by his identity disc, it was thought at first that he was the only occupant. The presence of a second crew-member was not suspected until a third hand was discovered.

In Britain, the fact that Gibson was missing was reported next day, and soon his death was presumed. But the only clue the Dutch had to the identity of the second man was a laundry tab on a sock, which they recorded in their report to the Dutch Red Cross as "Goy Gibsen". But the penny didn't drop. The engraving of the breastplate on the single coffin had been completed before the sock was discovered, and the coffin plate was then unscrewed and turned over, so that the name of a second man – presumably "Gibsen" – could be added. It was not until after the war that the Dutch realised who it was they had buried with James Warwick on that fatal day.

Eventually a more permanent memorial was erected to the two men, with Gibson's name given priority. There have been times since then when the grave has been neglected, but today the village of Steenbergen is a place of pilgrimage.

A further word about my friend Gerrit. "All in all," he says, "I was involved for 25 years in this work, the first five when still working for Naval Intelligence in my spare time and then as Recovery Officer, Royal Netherlands Air Force. In those years I was responsible for the recovery of some 130 World War 2 aircraft (or parts of), RAF, USAAF, and others – including in December 1985 what was left of Gibson's Mosquito.

"I always found this work very rewarding, being able to do something in return for what all those boys did for us.

"Believe me when I say that to be awarded the MBE (Member, Order of the British Empire) in 1979 was really great, also the KON, the Dutch Award (Knight in the Order of Orange Nassau).

"On our work, some documentary (video) films have been made, and one of them, *Some of Our Airmen are no Longer Missing*, is still available at the RAF Museum at Hendon."

Much has been said and written about the immediate casualties of the Dams' raid (which Gibson led) in human terms – some fortuitous, some inevitable – but the impact at a critical time remains undoubted.

## Chapter 7 – 'Jacko'

Norman Jackson, or 'Jacko', a self-assured flight engineer, had been exempt from military service before volunteering as a marine fitter, first on Sunderland flying-boats and then, when the new category was established in 1941 (to cover the new multi-engined bombers), as aircrew. Adopted as a child, he nevertheless – or perhaps consequentially – developed a strong family orientation, marriage followed early, and just before take-off, on this intended final sortie, he learned of the birth of his first child, a son. This, by mutual agreement, was according to plan. They intended to have many more children.

Here was another crew who despite many vicissitudes had vowed to stick together. Crew loyalty again. Their pilot's heavy-handedness on the controls they would put up with. They even boasted about it. He had other qualities. Even with their tour of operations nearly over, they had resolved to graduate together, after a rest, to 617 Squadron, instead of scattering to training units. Jackson, through doing an extra trip for a friend, had already done 30 trips, one ahead of his colleagues, but he wouldn't desert them for his 31st and their 30th.

Jackson and his bomb-aimer, Maurice Toft, had often discussed the feasibility of the circus acrobatics that Jackson might attempt, in emergency, to extinguish a fire in an engine, taking a parachute with him as a safety-net. It proved, as anyone would have forecast, suicidal. But, incredibly, he survived, after capture, to tell the tale. And earn an award. And father more children.

## Chapter 8 – The Air Cadet

Visiting the survivors of some of these highly decorated crews, I was sometimes in for a shock.

"Of course, you know what happened, don't you?" began the flight engineer in this story, Malcolm Mitchem, a thick-set West Countryman who was relishing his opportunity for an exposé.

"No, I don't. What?"

"We were shot down by our own side!"

How do you get a VC through being shot down by your own side? I had hit on something pretty dicey here, best left alone.

Eventually I asked: "How did it happen?"

When he told me the story, and when I read the account of the action written for me in blow-by-blow detail by Canadian bomb-aimer Allan Larden, and met the wizened but incomparable peacetime bus-conductor air gunner Jimmie Guy (by that time driving coaches round Britain's beauty spots), I no longer questioned the VC – nor the Conspicuous Gallantry Medal awarded to Larden, nor the Distinguished Flying Medals awarded to Mitchem and Guy.

## Chapter 9 – Bill Reid

How Bill Reid was unceremoniously grabbed by the Hon. Sir Ralph Cochrane (Air Vice-Marshal), for the fabled 617 Squadron (The Dam-Busters) as soon as he recovered from his VC wounds, is told here, also how he asked particularly for his bomb-aimer, Les Rolton, to go with him. "He's the best crew man I know." Who could resist such acclaim? Certainly not the 20-year-old, baby-faced Rolton, whose target photographs, whatever the carnage around him, somehow always managed to get results that confirmed the accuracy of his bombing. Later lost in another traumatic action which Reid miraculously survived, he had never thought, it seems, of not accompanying Reid to 617. Crew loyalty demanded it: they had been together since OTU.

Baldwin, the mid-upper gunner in the VC action, married three weeks earlier, sent me pen-pictures of all the crew, signing himself simply, "C. Baldwin". (He did, in his excellent account of the action, add "DFM".) "Rolton came from Romford and was a grammar-school boy, the baby of the crew, bit of a lad for the ladies but a very good man at his job." We then get the character vignette. "Sometimes he knew it, though." Cyril Baldwin, the only man to escape without a scratch, later fathered seven children.

Bill Reid protested, after my story was first published, that he thought perhaps I had exaggerated the frequency of the lapses into half-consciousness that I recorded. Not according to his crew.

## Chapter 10 – Target Amiens

From Frenchman Henri Moisan, of the *Organisation Civile et Militaire*, I was fortunate to get a full account of what it was like inside Amiens Jail on the morning of 18th February 1944. He was then a distinguished prisoner, under sentence of death. "I agree *grosso modo* with your relation," he wrote. He suggests one correction, "that the number of prisoners in the German part of the jail was very near the figure 196 that I saw myself on the wall, in the place where the daily number was written." I am happy to take his word for it.

But he adds: "It does not matter. What is more important is the question: Was it worth while to kill so many people, and to lose Pickard and Broadley, whose skill and gallantry would have been of such great value in future battles?"

"You know my opinion. It was a big and unlucky mistake, such as those occurring when artillery are firing on their own infantry. Such mistakes, numerous in all wars, are not spoken of afterwards. I understand that it was perhaps difficult to completely hide this event. But I think it improper to present it as a great achievement of war."

It remains a controversial issue. In fact, four planes only were lost, not as many as feared, and about 100 prisoners escaped, but bombs fell in the town, killing a number of prisoners and townspeople. Although the bitterness that might be expected seemed to have evaporated when the "battlefield" was visited by RAF veterans of the raid 48 years later, we must surely grant M. Moisan the last word.

# Index

205